**VIT.**

Igniting Your Organization's Spirit

For Marilyn —
a real joy
to meet you
Chuck
3/20/04

Marilyn —
You seem to bring real
Spirit to your work
and life — Good for you!
Mary 3-20-04

VITALITY

Igniting Your
Organization's Spirit

**Dr. Chuck Lofy and Dr. Mary Mead Lofy,
with John Lofy**

CRISP
PUBLICATIONS

Menlo Park, California

Vitality: Igniting Your Organization's Spirit

Dr. Chuck Lofy and Dr. Mary Mead Lofy, with John Lofy

Managing Editor: George Young

Editor: Sal Glynn

Cover and Book Design and Production: Fifth Street Design, Berkeley, CA

Library of Congress Cataloging-in-Publication Data

Lofy, Carl, 1931-
  Vitality : igniting your organization's spirit / by Carl Lofy and Mary
M. Lofy, with John Lofy.
      p. cm.
Includes bibliographical references and index.
  ISBN 1-56052-702-1 (pbk.)
  1. Organizational effectiveness. 2. Organizational change. 3. Trust.
4. Employee motivation. 5. Leadership. I. Lofy, Mary M., 1938- II.
Lofy, John, 1966- III. Title.
  HD58.9.L64 2004
  658.4'063--dc22
                          2003017936

ISBN 1-56052-702-1

03   04   05   06   07—10 9 8 7 6 5 4 3 2 1

AUTHORS' NOTE

Throughout *Vitality*, we use real-life stories from our consulting experience to illustrate our methods. Because our work delves into subjects like trust, conflict, and people's deepest thoughts and feelings, one of our methods is to ensure confidentiality. We have deliberately chosen not to identify any of the organizations mentioned in this book. We've also changed the names and a few identifying details of almost all the people whose work we describe here.

We often quote clients and workshop participants. These quotes are based on our memories, contemporaneous notes, and the memories of others who were present. They are accurate, but they are not verbatim transcripts.

In all other respects, the details of these stories are as complete and accurate as possible.

ACKNOWLEDGMENTS

Without the dozens of clients with whom we've worked over the past sixteen plus years, this book could not have been written. It has been our good fortune to work with smart, dedicated, and vitalized people around the country. Their stories, some of which are recounted here, provided us with interesting challenges, wonderful experiences, and, often, friendship. Their heroic efforts to bring vitality to their own organizations are a daily inspiration to us.

Along the way, we have formed friendships with many colleagues. Bill Bridges has always been a source of inspiration and strength. We also want to thank Babak Armajani, Larry Grant, and the other people of The Public Strategies Group, all of whom have offered us their enthusiastic support, instruction, and friendship.

More than anyone, our son John has been the catalyst whose sharp mind, writing ability, and caring spirit helped to create Vitality. It has been a singular privilege and joy to work with him.

Finally, we are deeply indebted to our family and friends without whose constant encouragement we'd not have completed this book.

For our grandchildren, Abe and Leo, David and Lila, with love

TABLE OF CONTENTS

INTRODUCTION

ordon Burns was worried. In the year since he'd taken over as president of an agricultural research firm, the company had been getting by just fine. Its scientific staff was stable and competent, and profits were steady, though slim. But for Burns, that was the problem. He'd come here from a dynamic corporation that was among the most successful in its field. It had been a competitive, nimble organization—not only profitable, but also a place where people enjoyed the work and devoted themselves to it enthusiastically. Employees trusted one another and collaborated effectively. They were loyal. Their success boosted their confidence, which in turn led to greater energy and success.

Here, on the other hand, everyone seemed content to simply survive. Burns thought that the company had fallen into a rut of complacency and mediocrity. They were happy to consider themselves second-tier.

Burns hoped to change that. He'd been hired to reinvigorate the company and bring it new prestige, and for a year he'd been bursting with visions of how to do it. He wanted to reconstitute the entire firm, and abolish outdated research divisions in favor of an inter-disciplinary approach. He wanted to hire the country's top researchers to carry out cutting-edge research and position the company as the best in the business. Sometimes his vision was so clear he could foresee the thrilling bustle in the hallways. He wanted to lead his company toward something most organizations want: high performance, greater productivity, good morale, and teamwork. He was after vitality.

What befuddled him was getting there. Burns hired us as consultants when his staff rejected his hopes for inter-disciplinary research. They preferred to protect their traditional turf and they scoffed at his desire to recruit top talent. "We're located in a backwater," they said, "and the real stars won't move here. Your best hope is to do what we've always done: pick up solid people and settle for second-best." The more he exhorted them toward greatness, the more they resisted. He started to force some reforms, but that only gave him the reputation as a bully, and he quickly realized that ramming his vision through without getting the staff on board would hardly inspire the excellence he sought.

This was why Burns worried. Would he really have to settle for mediocrity? He certainly didn't want to. He knew the satisfactions of succeeding alongside vibrant, engaged colleagues. Our help was engaged to help him forge ahead. These efforts would ultimately transform the staff, the structure of the organization, and Burns himself.

WHO SHOULD READ THIS BOOK?

Vitality is written for people who want to infuse vigor into their organizations. The material applies to all organizations: corporations, schools, churches, civic groups, government agencies, and others.

The book's purpose is two-fold. First, we explain what vitality is all about, and we show how vitality is affected by the forces of change, trust, and leadership. Each of these forces can crush or ignite organizational spirit. Second, we provide a practical method for enhancing vitality. This method uses change, trust, and leadership to revitalize an organization inside and out, from its day-to-day operations to the attitude and enthusiasm of its people.

Many of our consulting clients, like Gordon Burns, are trying to take their organization to the next level. They aren't satisfied with the status quo and they want to be excellent, not average; they want to boost profits, grow, or consolidate. Some have a vision of where they want to be, but they're not sure how to get there. Others find themselves stuck: they know they need to change, but they're not sure what they want. Still others are dealing with crises or stubborn problems, and want to

- Remain nimble and competitive in a tough business environment
- Get productivity out of a substantially downsized staff
- Retain good employees
- Change leadership
- Cope with a rapid growth or decline of profits, membership, or production
- Resolve conflict between labor and management (including unfinished business from past conflicts)

- Limit damage to organizational spirit caused by entrenched, negative members (many organizations have a few tenured or unfireable people who are nasty or cynical)
- Streamline a stifling bureaucracy
- Defuse a politicized climate in which quality and effectiveness fall prey to favoritism and grandstanding
- Improve lackluster performance
- Help people find meaning and gratification in their jobs even when they are overworked

Accomplishing these tasks is no easy matter. As Gordon Burns discovered, you can mandate policy, but you can't mandate creativity, confidence, and energy. This is the challenge of vitality. Vitality is about enhancing an organization's "life force," its dynamism and flexibility. Creating it requires dynamic, flexible methods, rather than rigid formulas. This book offers such a method.

We began writing this book during flush economic times, before the dot-com crash and the tragedy of September 11. Even as we considered the challenges organizations were facing, those challenges began to change. They became steeper and more grave. We wondered if we would need to adjust our message to accommodate these changing challenges. But we have been gratified to discover that, for us and our clients, the fundamentals of this book are even more relevant now than they were before. The world and the economy have plunged into uncertain times. The need for strong leadership, trust, and a deep understanding of change is greater now than it has been in years. Despite the new threats organizations face, we believe that vitality is just as important, and just as achievable, as it always was.

An organization may survive without vitality, though it's getting more difficult. Savage competition and a sluggish economy are just two threats to organizations. Even in good economic times, organizations have to contend with the movement of employees from one job to another, the incredible demands on people's time, and endless waves of change. All of these factors make it imperative that an organization brings out the very best in itself and its members.

There's also more to vitality. Even if becoming more dynamic and vital weren't a matter of survival, it's worth doing on its own account. Being part of a vitalized organization is its own reward. It is exciting, challenging, and even fun.

THE NATURE OF VITALITY

When you're in the presence of vitality, you know it. Writers like Tom Peters have talked about going into companies where they could "feel" the vibrant energy: "The language used in talking about people was different," Peters writes. "The love of the product and customer was palpable."[1] Vital organizations teem with innovation and cooperation. Their members are devoted and loyal, and they radiate enthusiasm. For people like Gordon Burns, the experience of working in a vitalized organization is so profound that it becomes a yardstick for measuring all later endeavors.

By its very definition ("the force of life," "dynamism," "energy"), vitality is something you can't really quantify. Where does it come from? How do you evoke it in an organization and how do you sustain it? For over three decades, we've tried to answer such questions. Our answers—which comprise this book—come from our experiences with organizations ranging from Fortune 500 companies to schools, churches, small businesses, and federal government agencies. One thing we know is that vitality cannot be standardized. It may look different from one organization to another. Vitality in a start-up or a non-profit may manifest itself as headlong enthusiasm. In a large corporation—with employees of diverse ages, values, and experiences—vitality might combine tradition with innovation. This book, therefore, deals with vitality as a process, rather than as a static condition. Its methods are adaptable to the particular needs and nature of your organization.

WHAT DOES VITALITY LOOK LIKE?

While vitality cannot be reduced to a simple formula, it does operate according to fundamental principles, which we describe in chapters one and two. Vitality is deeply affected by three basic factors—change, trust, and leadership—that can enhance or damage vitality. Finally, several "signal flags" indicate its presence. These flags can appear in any organization, whether it's a local school or a multinational conglomerate. The more you see these markers, the stronger is the vitality.

FIVE MARKERS OF VITALITY

1. *Spontaneous leadership*. This occurs when people assert leadership regardless of their position in the organization. "You can lead from anywhere," said a group made up of faculty members at a large, suburban middle school. The school was foundering in conflict—the new principal was unpopular, the veteran teachers cynical, and the building itself poorly configured. On their own initiative, several optimistic teachers began to discuss the problems. All agreed that something had to be done, but nobody knew what to do. Undaunted, they formed a "Next Step Task Force" to talk about the school community's concerns. They encouraged anyone who was interested to join them, reaching out in particular to the principal. Eventually they hired us as consultants and got the support of district officials for several crucial changes, but the most important factor in the school's turn-around was the faculty members' leadership.

2. *Stewardship*. Practicing stewardship means performing ordinary tasks to benefit an organization's broader community. Stewardship may involve simple tasks like washing the coffee maker or replenishing the photocopier. It might also mean serving on a committee or helping resolve conflicts among colleagues. Stewards keep their eyes open; when they see problems or opportunities to help, they step forward.

3. *Respect for difference*. There's a lot of talk about diversity these days, and many tests, like the Myers-Briggs Type Inventory, try to quantify the differences between people. In vitalized organizations, people go beyond the talk and the labels. They are not only aware of differences between people, they use differences as a resource. One particularly effective manager told us, "My job is to surround myself with people who know things I don't know and who think in ways I don't think." For him, bringing together different people increased his unit's strength and flexibility.

4. *Confidence*. Vitalized organizations believe in themselves and welcome

challenges. An executive once told us, "our management team is working so well that I don't believe there's a problem we can't handle." There was no cockiness in his demeanor, only self-assurance gained through experience and trust in his colleagues.

5. *Absence of ego.* Confidence does not imply arrogance. On the contrary, the people connected to confident organizations set aside their own egos for the greater good. They're team players with a respect for the truth: they give others credit when it's due, and are able to recognize and implement a good idea even if it's not their own.

Lack of ego also heightens the ability to absorb mistakes. Many organizations learn from mistakes, but the most innovative and daring do even more than that. They incorporate mistakes into their "organizational narrative." Mistakes become part of their identity—an inherent part of growth, and nothing to fear.

> ### TWO IMPORTANT QUESTIONS
>
> *How does an organization generate vitality?*
>
> *Once you have vitality, how do you maintain it?*

These markers of vitality are manifestations of one thing: *engagement.* They're the actions and attitudes of people who are deeply engaged in their organization. Organizations that want vitality have to get their people engaged. They must find, inspire, and retain dynamic, committed members, and they must create a climate where those people can thrive. That's easier said than done. Despite an organization's best efforts, it's common for people to *dis*engage, either by quitting, or by withdrawing their energy. Any number of things can break the link between an organization and its people. Seemingly minor problems can often be big deals to people, and alienate them from the organization. Changes can disorient people and make them "lose their place." Even enthusiastic members can wear out if they don't have the resources to accomplish their goals. All of this raises two practical questions. First, how does an organization without vitality get it? Second, once you have vitality, how do you maintain it? *Vitality* answers these questions.

VITALITY'S SPIRIT

Part One describes the fundamental components of vitality. It explains how people become engaged with organizations, and the ways organizations can encourage (or discourage) that engagement. We also describe the threats to vitality.

Vitalized organizations are marked by high levels of *spirit*. Everyone's heard the clichés about "school spirit" or "team spirit," where people "put their heart and soul" into an organization. Like many clichés, this one identifies real situations. People who get engaged are putting their intellects, emotions, values, and their bodies into the work. Many become so invested in what they're doing that it becomes a way of identifying themselves. "I'm a doctor," someone might say, or "I'm a Rotarian." These labels identify not only how she spends her time, but her outlook on the world, a whole way of seeing herself. When people get hooked up to the "right" job or the right organization—one that fits who they are and brings out the best in them—they get enormously energized. They put heart and soul into that job or organization. They assert spontaneous leadership and stewardship, and they spark others' spirits, spreading vitality throughout the organization.

CHANGE, TRUST, AND LEADERSHIP

In Part Two, we provide a method for dealing with the factors that can make or break vitality. Change, trust, and leadership are crucial to vitality. Each of them, managed well, can brighten any organization's spirit. If handled poorly, any can become a force that destroys vitality.

Change is as much a part of life these days as air. No one can afford to be bullied by change. It's crucial that organizations learn to make it a friend. When an organization changes well, it can overcome enormous obstacles and move to higher levels of development. Change allows growth, just as growth demands change.

On the other hand, once vitality has been sparked, changes can threaten it. We've all seen how unexpected crises and changes can hurt business. Even "good" changes can be a threat, like when an organization grows rapidly but loses the feeling that it's a tight-knit family. Change, in short, can be vitality's greatest ally or its greatest enemy.

The same is true of trust and leadership. Either can tip an organization toward greater vitality or away from it. Organizations need trust to ensure innovation, cooperation, and engagement, and they need strong leadership to guide them toward greater spirit.

The chart below (figure i-1) shows how change, trust, and leadership affect vitality.

Figure i–1

FACTOR	**POTENTIAL TO INCREASE VITALITY**	**POTENTIAL TO DAMAGE VITALITY**
Change **Chapters 4–5**	Change is the water organizations drink. It is omnipresent and continuous. As an ally, it can rejuvenate an organization by moving it to a new developmental level, by clearing out "dead wood," or by reforming practices that no longer work.	When people are already engaged, change can make them feel anxious or confused, sapping their spirits. At the same time, failure to change can lead to stagnation and malaise.
Trust **Chapter 6**	Trust is the decisive element for vitality. When people feel safe, they invest spirit into their organization. They are honest, venture innovative ideas, and work well in teams.	Distrust kills vitality, as the case of Andersen Accounting demonstrated. In a climate of distrust, people try to protect themselves. They withdraw. They stop innovating and taking risks, they avoid conflict resolution, and their interest in being "team players" withers.
Leadership **Chapter 7**	Dynamic leaders can spark vitality in even the most apathetic organization. Several of the most dynamic leaders we've met, moreover, were custodians, technicians, junior faculty, and support staffers. Eliciting such spontaneous leadership is absolutely crucial to vitality.	It's no secret that people in power have the ability to make others' lives miserable. Intentionally or not, leaders can create or perpetuate harmful forms that impede, rather than encourage, their organization's effectiveness and spirit.

At the core of Part Two is our technique for using change, trust, and leadership to create vitality. We call this technique "Clarification" because it *clarifies* what is really going on in an organization. Clarification is more than just fact-gathering, it is a way of learning. This technique explores an organization's hidden dynamics—its history and culture, unfinished business, and the true thoughts and feelings of its people. Moreover, it engages people. Clarification empowers them to participate in making their organization a better place to be. It encourages stewardship and leadership, builds confidence, and helps people understand one another's similarities and differences.

> Clarification *is the core of Part Two. This method of learning brings the members of an organization together. The process builds trust and leadership, and guides organizations through change.*

Each of the chapters in Part Two delineates the basic processes of Clarification. Chapters four and five deal with change, chapter six with trust, and chapter seven with leadership. Their lessons overlap, and each subject teaches something about the others. For instance, changing well demands trust. Trust generates innovation and change, and without leadership, change and trust are left to chance, and vitality is jeopardized.

WHO WE ARE

For years, most recently as organizational consultants, we have been implementing the ideas and methods of *Vitality* in real organizations. Our goal is to spark vitality in organizations enduring difficult change or serious conflict, or that are ready to take the next step in their development. We achieve this goal in two ways. First, we help people understand how change, trust, and leadership affect vitality. Second, we provide a method to manage change, build trust, and develop leadership in ways that bring vitality about.

Many of our clients tell us that our work is set apart by its depth, and we suspect that's because we attend to the inner lives of organizations, the dynamics that ordinarily remain hidden from view. We've been business owners and managers, a university administrator, an elected official, a professor, a counselor, and parents. Early in our lives, Chuck was a Jesuit priest and Mary a Dominican nun. These broad experiences enable us to find fundamental truths that apply to all organizations. In our jobs, people tell us their deepest hopes, frustrations, and fears. From years of deep listening, we have discovered basic principles about how people in organizations interact and what causes them to feel alive and engaged.

These principles make *Vitality* flexible and broadly relevant. The material here applies equally well to personal lives, rural agricultural cooperatives, and Fortune 500 companies. Our client list is diverse, including corporations such as AT&T, 3M, and General Electric; educational institutions ranging from the Minneapolis school district to the University of Nevada–Reno; churches of all denominations; and government agencies. *Vitality* brings together this panoply of experience.

Vitality is not only a book of ideas. Our livelihood depends on providing our clients with practical, effective methods. As we've developed this material over the years, we've had to discard dozens of ideas that seemed good in theory but fell apart in practice. What remains—this book—has proven itself in the real world. It works.

GETTING THERE

Any organization can achieve vitality, but doing so demands dedicated, ongoing effort. This book won't give you a quick fix. The methods here attend to core issues like building trust among people with different views, dealing with revolutionary change, and helping individuals to step forward and make a difference. They require real dedication, and sometimes demand a whole new way of thinking. Those who follow the journey to the end, however, will find it worth the effort.

For Gordon Burns, the trip was particularly perilous. By the time he asked us to consult with his firm, relations between him and some staff members had soured so badly they could barely speak to one another. The first step was clearly to re-establish trust and communication.

During a trust-building workshop with the research staff, in which people were allowed and expected to be fully honest, criticism piled up around Burns. He'd heard much of it already. He was short-tempered and dictatorial, they said, and he didn't listen to the staff's opinions. Someone also revealed that the former CEO, who retired but still lived in town, had been bad-mouthing Burns since before he'd arrived. Burns listened all day long, patiently considering the criticism, trying to learn from it.

The criticism also angered and hurt him. The next day, when it was his turn to respond, he apologized for having acted, as he put it, like "the meanest SOB in the county." But, he added, he believed that he'd been forced into that position. He'd never acted like a dictator in his previous jobs. Maybe it was the former CEO's gossip preceding him, maybe it was that he laid out his vision clearly enough—but from the beginning, he said, he'd felt unwelcome and disparaged. "I suppose I figured, 'If they think I'm such a tyrant, then I will be.'"

Some of what he said seemed to surprise Burns himself. Certainly this was new to the staff, who glimpsed the human side of him for the first time. His honesty and willingness to hear the researchers' criticism went a long way toward opening communication. During later sessions, trust clearly began to deepen. People connected.

With trust improving, they began talking about the company's future. Burns was able to loosen the grip on some of his personal visions, while the staff began to appreciate his ambitious goals. Burns got everyone to agree that new discoveries had permanently shifted their field of agricultural science. Genetics, bioengineering, and related technologies had become more important than the old distinctions between, for instance, plant and animal science. Yet the company was still divided into departments based on the old distinctions. Burns wanted to abolish the traditional departments and create an inter-disciplinary structure to capitalize on the new scientific landscape, but many staff members wanted to keep the old departments (and the perks like managerial positions that went with it).

The transformation required more than a year of hard discussions and difficult choices. Eventually, as a group and by consensus, they reinvented the company. Later in the book, we'll describe the methods they used. For now, it suffices to say the old divisions were thrown out, much as Burns wanted. The changes, though they seemed inevitable in hindsight, were revolutionary, and the company marketed its new structure to top scientists in the field. When those people visited, they found not a backwater but a firm where researchers were performing cutting-edge work and, most important, where they did so with enthusiastic teamwork. Everyone wanted to work there, and before long the firm was receiving national attention. It exemplified the words "thriving" and "vitality." Burns had achieved his vision.

ENDNOTES

1. Peters, Thomas J., and Robert H. Waterman, Jr. *In Search of Excellence* (New York: Harper & Row, 1982), pg. 16.

Part One:

INSIDE/OUTSIDE

1 ✳ Form and Spirit

e recently worked with a group that epitomized vitality. A committee had been assigned to "reinvent" a corporate division. The organization's executives had created several such task forces, one for each aspect of its operations. This group took on customer relations, and its nine members dove into the task. Before setting out to gather data on the firm's customer relations, they took time to fully prepare themselves: they did team-building exercises, discussed their own experiences of receiving customer service, and trained for the interviews they were about to conduct with customers and front-line employees across the country. Then they gathered information and suggestions as fast as they could. They believed in their work and they loved their boss, a witty, driven leader who encouraged them to improvise and think creatively. "Live the question," he admonished them. "Don't be afraid to be confused. Your questions will lead you to the heart of the matter."

Working there, they told us later, was wonderful. "We have an incredible degree of everyday freedom," one said. "And we've come up with some really fresh approaches to our work."

They felt totally engaged. "We work really well together as a team," one said. Another added, "I've never laughed so much on the job." To a person, they confided that they were deeply grateful they could work there. "This is the best job I've ever had," said one man. "It's brought out the best in me. I've made a difference."

The work they produced was fresh and important. When the company implemented the group's recommendations, its customer satisfaction jumped. The group, in short, had a good time doing excellent work. Everyone, from the employees to the customers to the company as a whole, benefited. This is what happens when an organization has vitality.

Where does such vitality come from? How do you inspire and sustain it? In the introduction, we listed several markers of vitality and noted that what these traits share in common is *engagement*. When people become deeply involved with their organization, investing "heart and soul," they vitalize it. Think of the parent, for example, who gets involved with her child's school by joining the PTA, chaperoning the prom, or raising funds for a team or club. She is engaged in the school, helping it reach its goals. The school, in fact, depends on the engagement of hundreds of people: students, teachers, administrators, and the taxpaying community. Each of these people gives something to the school. Without them, it's an empty building.

> *Vitality arises from the engagement of people in an organization.*

People have always "given" themselves to organizations, and organizations only survive thanks to their dedication. Virtually every aspect of an organization, from operations to customer service to quality control, teamwork, and innovation—depend on the commitment of people. People will only engage if the organization rewards their efforts. These rewards can be tangible, such as a paycheck and benefits, but they can also be intangible. People can be rewarded with the feeling that they are doing something important, they are helping others, they're learning and growing, or being challenged to deploy all their talents. All these and more are the rewards people get from being engaged in organizations, whether that's on the job, or in their church, school, or civic group. Vitality comes about when people engage in an organization, and both they and the organization become better for it.

REWARDING ENGAGEMENT

Engaging people is crucial to an organization's success, but it's difficult to do. For instance, several companies we consult with are asking employees to do jobs once handled by three or four people. Time is short for most people, both at home and at work. Just getting the job done is tough enough; making it exciting can seem impossible. Employers ask a lot from people. When they don't reward employees' engagement, the employees *dis*engage. They stop giving themselves to their work. They just "get by" on the job, or they quit altogether. Then it's even harder to get people re-engaged.

This happened at a software company with which we consulted. It had been growing successfully for several years when profits and new product creation sagged. The staff turnover rate jumped. When managers surveyed current and past employees to determine why so many of them were leaving, the employees said they were disillusioned. As the company had grown, they had ceased to feel "part of things." The company paid them well, they said, but drove them too hard and encouraged internal competition at the expense of cooperation. They felt isolated and undervalued. Even those who hadn't quit felt burned out.

Turnover is an expected part of business, but the levels at this firm were exceptionally high. Of even greater concern was the burnout of those employees who'd chosen to stay around. Lethargic software writers weren't going to help the company compete.

To restore the energy, productivity, and creativity that marked the company's greatest success, management began revamping the company's entire culture. They improved employee perks and gave their people much more decision-making power. They created a "Year of the Employee," investing in their peoples' training and well-being. Before long, they turned the losses around, and even hired back some former employees.

The dot-com crash challenged the company further, but thanks to their revitalized people, they weathered the storm better than most. They continue to look for ways to engage their members at deeper levels, to bring out their best and reward it not only with money and benefits, but with a vitalized, exciting environment. In such a situation, people put time and energy into their work, and the organization puts time and energy into them.

> *People engage in an organization when the organization rewards their engagement.*

This dynamic exchange is vitality. To say it another way: vitality arises when an organization and its people "fit." Each gets and gives something essential.

Vitality is largely self-sustaining. When people are engaged and enthusiastic, others follow. Together they solve problems and address threats to their cohesion. They overcome enormous obstacles, ranging from logistical problems to their own fears. The more success they achieve, the more people engage. Everyone gets swept up in the forward momentum.

LOSING VITALITY: THE PRINCIPAL'S TALE

Unfortunately, just as vitality is self-sustaining, so is the lack of vitality. When people disengage from an organization, they can open a vitality drain that is very hard to plug.

A school district was embroiled in labor conflict. The faculty had been working without a contract for five years; animosity between the teachers and administrators was so ferocious that the state legislature finally stepped in and forced both sides to accept binding arbitration. As a parallel to the arbitration, we were called in to help rebuild trust between the parties. During a workshop that included representatives of the faculty, staff, administration, and school board, one of the school principals made a confession.

"For me," he began, "the problems began during the strike we had eight years ago. I wasn't on the negotiating team and had nothing to do with writing the new contract, but with all the conflict, I wanted to bring everybody together. I hosted a barbecue for the faculty of my school. My wife and I worked for three days, cleaning the house, shopping, setting up games for everyone to play...." His voice began to shake. "...and the union called a boycott. No one showed up at the barbecue. We sat around waiting, and no one even called to say why they weren't coming."

He glared at the faculty members. "I confess that ever since that day, I've hated you. And I'll tell you what else. On that day I stopped being the educational leader of the school. I stopped putting forth creative ideas. I just took care of the tasks in front of me."

The principal's disengagement clearly damaged his school's vitality. Not only did he fail to move the school forward, he allowed it to founder in conflict. In situations like this, one key person can hurt an entire organization's vitality. More and more people disengage, and a climate of apathy and cynicism takes hold. This climate builds on itself until the whole culture is devitalized—and *devitalizing*. It robs newcomers of their personal vitality. One woman told us how her Fortune 500 employer sapped her energy. She had joined the company bursting with ideas. "I came in here like a hundred watt light bulb," she said, but whenever she expressed enthusiasm, her colleagues just shrugged and went on with what they'd been doing. After a while, she stopped trying. "Now," she confessed, "I'm more like a twenty-watt bulb that flickers on every once in a while." She had become another disengaged employee.

VITALITY ARISES WHEN FORM AND SPIRIT ENHANCE EACH OTHER

Engagement is a two-way street. People will engage in something only if it rewards that engagement. There is the thing that you engage *in*, and the thing that actually does the engaging. Engagement is like investing. In investment, you put your money into stocks or bonds. With engagement, you invest time, energy, intelligence, and emotion into your activities.

We call these two halves of engagement *spirit* and *form*.[1] Engagement occurs when people invest their "spirits" into "forms." By spirit, we don't mean "soul" or anything religious. We use "spirit" as shorthand for people's ideas, emotions, values, and energy.

> *To thrive, an organization needs effective forms and vibrant spirit.*

By "form" we mean an organization's structures: its buildings, management chart, human resource policies, the goods or services it produces, and its workday schedule (see figure 1–1 for more). Forms give an organization shape.

Figure 1–1

FORMS COMMONLY FOUND IN ORGANIZATIONS

Buildings	Goods or services provided	Unions
Benefits packages	Hiring/firing procedures	Computer networks
Management structure	Pay scale	Accounting system
Mission statement	Logo and trademark	Dress code
Advertisements	Work hours	Manufacturing lines

The U.S. Army slogan, "Be all you can be," offers a good example of how form and spirit interact. The slogan implies that the Army will give you the forms of tools, training, and discipline; these will draw out and enhance your best qualities—your *spirit*. Your spirit engages with the forms, and everyone benefits. The Army gets engaged, well-trained soldiers who make the Army's forms work, and the soldiers get an interesting tour of duty and training for the future, meanwhile growing into the best person they can be. This is the goal, anyway.

When form and spirit work together, as in figure 1–2, vitality arises. Similarly, when form and spirit disconnect, vitality falters. That's what happened with the school principal. His spirit had been invested in the form of being "educational leader" of the school. After the barbecue conflict, he withdrew his spirit. He disinvested from the form, and the school's vitality suffered.

Figure 1–2

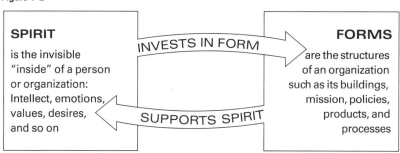

Spirit can be invested into form, like when you put "heart and soul" into your business. Form can support and develop spirit, as when a school educates a student, a church nurtures a believer, or a business challenges and trains an employee.

This relationship between form and spirit is at the heart of vitality. To thrive, an organization needs good forms and strong spirit. Good forms (such as a clear accounting system, a safe building, and a fair personnel policy) sustain day-to-day operations. The organization's spirit (the energy, ideas, and commitment of its members) makes things happen, and moves the organization forward. Moreover, strong spirit makes better forms, and good forms improve spirit.

Because form and spirit are the heart of vitality, we'll examine them here in greater depth.

FORM

The psychologist Rollo May says that humans have a natural instinct for order, a "passion for form."[2] By our definition, "form" is anything that structures people's lives. A simple example would be the rules of a game, which establish limits within which play proceeds. If you stop following the rules, trouble arises. When our kids were little, they played football in our front yard. They started each game so eagerly that rules were never established beforehand. When the competition heated up, they fought over which tree marked the end zone or whether the sidewalk was out of bounds, and inevitably someone would come into the house crying. Without rules, the game was *formless* and impossible to play.

Broadly defined, forms can be just about any kind of structure. They can be *physical objects*—anything from a city to a building to someone's body. Clothes are forms, so are dental instruments. Forms can also be sets of *guidelines* or *expectations*, such as rules of grammar or etiquette, a college's graduation requirements, or a job's position description. Such forms are often created by a contract—usually explicit, but often unwritten or even unspoken. A college student, for instance, is given explicit instructions to follow if she wants to earn a diploma. If she wants to make sure she gets a good *education* as well as a diploma, she'll have to follow some additional, unwritten guidelines to make sure she takes the right combination of classes, and to pick up some real-life experience along the way. Another example: a marriage is a combination of explicit legal requirements and expectations, and a whole lot of agreements (some explicit, some not) that the couple

> *SOME TYPES OF FORMS*
>
> • *Physical objects*
>
> • *Rules, laws, guidelines, and expectations*
>
> • *Habits and routines*
>
> • *Groups*
>
> •*Relationships*

works out along the way. In these cases, the form's boundaries are partly explicit, and partly unspoken.

Habits and *traditions* are forms—when people say "we've always done things that way," they're talking about forms. *Groups* and *relationships* can even be forms. Most groups are comprised of specific people with specific functions. If the group's boundaries and expectations are well established, they are a type of form.

Forms overlap and many forms contain smaller forms inside them. A corporation is comprised of forms as varied as labor unions, factories, and shareholder meetings (figure 1–2). It is affected by outside forms: its suppliers, the economy as a whole, and governments five or five thousand miles away. Forms are like mountain climbers tied to a survival line: where one goes, others will follow.

What Forms Do

There's a lot to be said for forms. They create *predictability* and *clarity*, and set *routines*, *boundaries*, and *expectations*. We generally know what to expect when we come to work. There's usually a particular building in a particular place. For many people, their job has routine tasks to be accomplished; others may have less predictable day-to-day duties, but they probably know their role in the organization and the parameters they should follow in deciding what to do and how to do it. Even a very flexible form like telecommuting requires some degree of structure and discipline to be effective. In short, good forms tell us where we are and what we should do next.

> *Good forms tell us where we are and what to do next. Some forms even tell us who we are.*

Forms also make the world *safer*. Traffic laws channel what could be freeway mayhem into (usually) safe travel. Forms *create efficiency* by matching certain needs to particular locations—there are kitchens for cooking and bedrooms for sleeping; hospitals take care of sick people while bowling alleys cater to bowlers. By centralizing these activities, forms save time and consolidate resources.

Forms are most effective when they set clear, fair, and consistent boundaries that give people enough leeway to accomplish their goals. More than that, forms can also help people find creative ways to reach their goals. Think of the rule that basketball players must dribble the ball. That's a form. Instead of making the game boring, the rule creates excitement as players dribble behind their backs and between their legs to avoid the defense. The form makes demands; meeting those demands stretches players' abilities and makes them grow.

Forms help people, but they can also hurt. Some forms even attack spirit. In his essay "The Ethics of Living Jim Crow," Richard Wright (author of *Black Boy* and *Native Son*) describes the oppressive forms that arose from racial inequality in the 1940s and

> *The best forms give us an ample space for creativity within clear, fair, and consistent boundaries.*

1950s. "One day," he writes, "I stepped into an elevator with my arms full of packages. I was forced to ride with my hat on (though it would have been polite to take it off indoors). Two white men stared at me coldly. Then one of them very kindly lifted my hat and placed it upon my armful of packages. Now the most accepted response for a Negro to make under such circumstances is to look at the white man out of the corner of his eye and grin. To have said: 'Thank you!' would have made the white man *think* that you *thought* you were receiving from him a personal service. For such an act I have seen Negroes take a blow in the mouth."[3]

Two important forms appear in this passage. The first is the requirement to remove a hat when indoors, a matter of etiquette expected of every man. The second form is the black man's "accepted response" of grinning surreptitiously. Both forms are designed to signal respect, but the sly grin demanded of Wright was something required only of blacks. It was designed to keep him in an inferior position and demeaned his spirit. Moreover, that grin re-established the white man's power, while still allowing the white man to feel generous and friendly. The real function of this form was to break African Americans' spirit and to elevate whites'. Sadly, the world has no shortage of forms that are similarly hostile to spirit.

Unlike these oppressive forms, good forms reward people's engagement. Besides the rewards of safety, predictability, efficiency, and clear expectations, forms can actually *help people define themselves*. Most of us derive our identities from forms like our nationality, ethnic background, and jobs; by whether we're parents, spouses, single, liberal or conservative, religious or secular, male or female, and so on. All of these labels represent forms. Marriage is a form with boundaries and expectations; so is parenthood. Religions are forms centered on spiritual beliefs. People engage with such forms at a much deeper level than they do with other forms. They put their hearts and minds into these forms. They invest their spirits.

> *Some forms—like slavery and dictatorship—crush spirit.*

SPIRIT

Most people have had the happy experience of being part of a "spirited" organization. They talk about school or team spirit, or maybe refer to a particularly spunky person as someone with "great spirit."

We use spirit to refer to the intangible "inside" of a person or organization. Spirit is emotion, intellect, and values. It is the culture or atmosphere of a place. (Again, we do not use "spirit" in the religious sense—though it can be read that way.)

Spirit is difficult to define because you can't really touch it. Maybe the best way to define spirit is to consider how it differs from form. One example is the old proverb about "making a house a home." A house is a form, a structure. Turning a house into a "home" where you feel safe, comfort-

> *Spirit is the "inside" of a person, organization, or system. Thoughts, feelings, values, culture— all part of spirit.*

able, and happy, requires an investment of spirit. You "make it your own," and "put your heart into it." The house becomes a home because it reflects your spirit—your taste, values, memories, aspirations, and traditions.

Another example is the distinction between "the letter of the law" and "the spirit of the law." Laws are forms, and when we follow "the letter of the law," we strictly adhere to the law's form. There are times when enforcing the letter of the law seems unfair and unjust, like when a confessed murderer gets off on a legal technicality, or when people who commit minor infractions suffer heavy punishment. At such times, we appeal to the spirit of the law, which is Justice.

Laws in most countries are not written for their own sake. Their purpose is to create Justice. Laws are the form that make the spirit of justice possible, and we measure the quality of laws by the degree to which they manifest Justice. The vitality of the legal system, moreover, depends on whether justice is present. Laws without justice are arbitrary proclamations; form without spirit has little meaning or vitality.

> *Spirit makes a house a home. The "spirit of the law" is Justice; the spirit of Justice gives life to the "letter of the law," which is a form..*

Spirit is the *core* of a person or system, its essence and reason for being. While form is structure, spirit is intangible. The only way to identify spirit is to "feel" its presence in a form.

How do you "feel" spirit? Think about meetings, which are forms. You *know*, when you're in one, whether or not the meeting has spirit. If it doesn't, it drones boringly along. If it contains spirit, people are *engaged*. They feel strongly and think hard about the topic at hand. Whether they argue or cooperate, they're "there." There's something at stake for them; the conversation matters. Such a meeting exemplifies vitality.

VITALITY REQUIRES BOTH SPIRIT AND FORM

An organization can get by without effective forms and survive without strong spirit, but to achieve real vitality, it needs both. We know the director of a nonprofit organization. When she took over, the place's spirit was high, but its forms were a shambles. Because the former director had been a scientist and not a trained administrator, basic forms had languished. Paperwork was months out of date. Grant proposals went unsent because the director hadn't kept up with the deadlines. Audits and financial statements were three years in arrears.

Fortunately for the organization, a group of spirited employees had kept the place afloat. When the budget periodically collapsed, some of them would work without pay. Others asserted spontaneous leadership by creating a committee to manage administrative crises, but they could see that their enthusiasm wouldn't save the organization. They spent so much time putting out fires that they neglected their own work, and the effort sapped their energy. Despite the employees' help, several donors became so fed up with the director's incompetence they withheld further funding. Several said that they would reopen the spigot if he was replaced, but for now, the organization's existence was in doubt.

All the spirit in the world can't help an organization without good forms. Moreover, the problems with the forms damaged spirit: the employees exhausted themselves trying to take care of the organization, and the director suffered from their distrust.

A nonprofit lost vitality by having ineffective forms. A school lost it when key people withdrew their spirits.

The board hired a new director, a woman with strong business and administrative skills, to establish order. She spent the next year setting up systems for accounting, budgeting, information technology, and fundraising. With staff input, she rewrote the outdated policy manual. She built benefits packages from the ground up. As she re-established strong forms, donors began to trust the organization again, and funds began to flow back in.

If the nonprofit suffered from poor forms, the problem at the school with the disengaged principal was that it lacked spirit. The school's forms worked fine. Indeed, as the principal himself said, all he worked on were the forms. He signed papers and paid the rent and made sure students graduated, but the school spirit turned acidic, full of cynicism and distrust.

Just as the neglected forms of the nonprofit hurt people's spirit, the negative spirit at the school began to take its toll on forms. Most important, it made one of the most basic forms—a faculty contract—almost impossible to create. Animosity tainted every negotiation.

In the end, both organizations fixed their problems. The nonprofit's new director revamped all the forms. She restored the organization to fiscal health and rebuilt relationships with funders and the community. At the school, the principal's admission opened a dialogue that eventually resolved the conflicts, and a new spirit of cooperation arose.

Vitality suffers if either form or spirit is not strong. When form and spirit build on each other, vitality results. People get enthusiastic about engaging in their work, and they create ways to do it better. A culture of trust, confidence, and pride arises; everyone pulls together toward common goals of success.

HOW VITALITY WORKS

Vitality arises from the dynamic interplay of form and spirit. The basic pattern of vitality can be illustrated like this:

Figure 1–3

People invest spirit into form, making the form work.

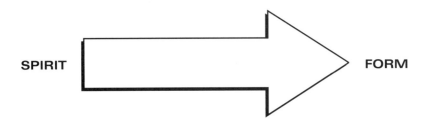

SPIRIT   FORM

When people trust that an organization will reward their investment, they begin to invest spirit. They get engaged. That engagement makes the form "work" (figure 1–3). It transforms the school building into an educational center. It makes a house a home, and animates laws with justice.

Figure 1–4

Good forms reward investment by providing an arena for growth, as well as boundaries that offer safety, predictability, and efficiency.

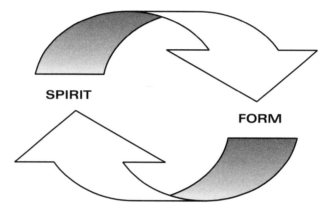

In turn, the forms reward people's investment (figure 1–4). The form makes people safe. It develops their abilities, improves their efficiency, and makes them feel at home. Good forms give people a sense of identity.

Figure 1–5

When people find that their engagement is rewarded, they continue to invest spirit, and a dynamic interaction arises between form and spirit: vitality.

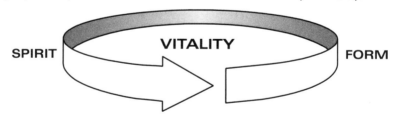

Because the form fosters their spirits, people engage even more deeply. They commit more completely to the form. If the form is flawed, they try to fix it.

A flow of energy arises between the organization's forms and people's spirit (figure 1–5). Each enhances the other; they build on each other. The organization itself takes on a spirit of its own, created out of the energy and relationships of its members. This is vitality.

We know from experience that vitality is within the reach of any organization, but before we discuss its implementation, we need to discuss some of the inner workings of spirit and form.

UNEXPECTED CONNECTIONS BETWEEN FORM AND SPIRIT

When one of our sons was in high school, Chuck went on a spring cleaning spree. He vacuumed, dusted, and scrubbed the whole house. When he got to our son's room, he attacked the piles of dirty clothes, stacked books and games, and old pizza crusts tucked under the bed. He threw away all sorts of junk and polished the room to an immaculate shine.

You can guess what happened. Our son was furious. Not only had his father gone digging around in his private stuff, he complained, he had also thrown out his favorite pair of shoes.

Chuck was baffled. His favorite shoes? He'd only thrown away two lace-less, decaying tennis shoes barely held together by ragged duct tape. "Exactly!" our son roared. "You know how long it took to break those shoes in?" Even his friends admired the shoes. What seemed like trash turned out to be a symbol of our son's autonomy, privacy, and (most bewildering of all) keen fashion sense. The apparently worthless *form* of the shoes was actually a crucial manifestation of his *spirit*.

People often invest spirit in unlikely forms, like shoes and accounting systems.

Our family still jokes about the misunderstanding, but it taught us that form and spirit are connected in unexpected, invisible ways. It would be wonderful if an organization could simply say, "we'll foster spirit with good forms." It's much more complicated than that, because when the hidden connections between form and spirit aren't recognized, even well-meaning actions can result in lasting conflict. In other words, you don't have to be hostile to spirit to damage it.

LOSING GOOD FORMS: THE BANKERS' STORY

Spirit's hidden connection to form can have very high stakes. A few years ago, we consulted with a successful regional bank. Over the previous two years, it had acquired several smaller institutions and had nearly tripled the number of its branch offices. Tom Grand, the CEO, asked us for help because despite the bank's success, the management and staff didn't seem happy. On the contrary, they were irritable and apathetic.

We began with a two-day workshop for the bank's branch presidents and other administrators. Our goal was to discover the sources of the discontent. To achieve this goal, we needed to create an environment where people could speak honestly about the effects of the recent changes on their jobs, the bank itself, and their personal lives. Early on, we set out a "contract for safety"—an agreement that the participants could speak freely without fear of management's reprisal (or remain silent if they chose), and that all participants would protect one another's anonymity.

As we sipped coffee in the hallway during a break, one of the branch presidents shuffled up and murmured, "Even with these agreements, you're not going to get anywhere with this group. No one here says what they think in front of the CEO."

We went ahead anyway and split the participants into small groups, and asked them to discuss how the bank's changes affected them personally. When they reported back, it was clear that the first two groups had not talked openly. They simply presented laundry lists of recent changes in forms, without describing the changes' effects. We began to believe the branch president had been right until we came to the third group. One of the presidents stood up.

"I'm going to say the most important thing in this workshop all day," Martin announced. "I noticed when we were talking that no one was saying what they really meant. Well, I was sitting there, and I figured, I'm 64 years old. Nobody's going to fire me for telling the truth."

It turned out that Martin was in the same group as Grand, the CEO. He turned to Grand and said, "Our presidents' meetings are useless. There's seventeen branch presidents sitting there, going through stacks of financial reports and meanwhile I feel like I'm covered in blood. My accountants are frustrated because of this new accounting system nobody understands, and we're getting audited on it. I don't know what to tell my accountants when they ask my advice. My loan officers are upset because they can't approve large loans on their own authority anymore. They have to call this guy Gottfried in the central office. I don't even know who Gottfried is. None of these problems are ever addressed, and instead we waste meeting time on trivia. The meetings are a bunch of BS."

Everyone was stunned. It was silent for a while, then Grand managed to thank Martin for speaking up. He turned to another of the branch presidents. "Lester," he said. "Do *you* think our presidents' meetings are a bunch of BS?"

Unlike Martin, Lester wasn't 64 and unconcerned about being fired. He was 36, with a family to feed. Everyone waited while he scratched his elbow, tapped his knee, and opened his mouth a few times, only to close it. Finally he said to Grand, "Except when *you're* talking, yes, they're a waste of time."

Grand laughed at this and everyone relaxed. More important, they started to speak openly. They described the aggravation of working longer hours, the difficulty of understanding new procedures, and their sadness that the bank no longer felt like a family.

The conversation, especially for Grand, wasn't much fun. He thought that the employees only needed a pep rally, but now he had to face their anger, frustration, and anxiety. In situations like this, there's always a danger that people will make unreasonable attacks, pout, or become defensive. In later chapters, we'll talk about how to deal with these problems, but for now we only need to observe that the truth had come out. Painful as the process was for Grand—and risky as it had been for Martin and Lester—if no one had spoken up, the consequences for the bank would have been grievous.

The connection between form and spirit can be very difficult to see. In this situation, the changes didn't seem dramatic. Accountants had to adjust to a new system, and loan officers had to get approval to loan large sums. It's easy to understand why they might not like the new rules—their autonomy was threatened—but Martin's reaction was more surprising. For him to say that he felt "covered in blood" seemed melodramatic. It implied that he felt beaten up, angry, and, strangely enough, guilty. How could his reaction be so extreme?

Martin had always identified himself as someone who could solve problems as they arose. That's how he saw his spirit. Now here he was, a wise and experienced bank president who couldn't help his employees, and couldn't understand the new systems himself. It violated his sense of who he was. What's more, Martin and the other branch presidents sat through meetings where they couldn't raise important issues. Their talents as problem-solvers, managers, and leaders languished. None of the bank's new forms rewarded the executives' investment. Even more, the system simply didn't *allow* them to invest their spirits. These forms were not safe, efficient, or clear, and rather than giving people a sense of identity, the forms took their identities away.

Does this affect the bottom line? An organization whose highest officers believe that their meetings are "BS" and who describe themselves as "covered in blood" is not positioned for long-term success.

INVESTMENT IN FORM

Our son with his sneakers and Martin with his bank systems had invested their spirits into their respective forms, but how do you predict which forms will matter to someone? The truth is, you often can't. Form and spirit can be connected just about anywhere, with varying degrees of attachment. No one puts spirit into every form he or she encounters. With some forms—toothpaste, say—investing spirit would be downright embarrassing. Other forms can make you very enthusiastic, but only for a short time. Still others seem so right that you're willing to commit yourself to them for years, possibly your whole life. If we paint these degrees of involvement on a spectrum, they look like this (figure 1–6):

Figure 1–6

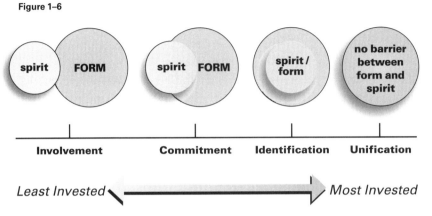

Involvement   Commitment   Identification   Unification

Least Invested ← ——————————→ *Most Invested*

Involvement is when a person lends a form time and energy for a short duration. For instance, every year a friend of ours participates in a few charity events like the "Race for a Cure" fund-raiser for breast cancer research. She plays a small, limited part. She cares about the issue, but her spirit isn't deeply invested in the form.

Commitment involves a promise to *continue* to be involved. This is often the level of investment people have with their jobs. Commitment shows up in other ways, too. Another woman we know has helped organize the "Race for a Cure" for several years now, ever since her sister died of breast cancer. The cause matters deeply to her, and she feels a strong desire to make the race happen. She does more than participate in the form, she helps create it.

Identification occurs when a person feels defined by the form. The form gives her an identity, and when she invests spirit, she helps create the form. In marriage, people usually develop an identity as a spouse. The form defines them. At the same time, they invest spirit into the form of the marriage, which makes the form work. The more they give to the form, the more the form defines who they are.

The same sort of identification with form often happens with work. Primo Levi, a Jewish chemist and writer who survived a year in Auschwitz during World War II, describes how Jews were forced into slave labor in the concentration camps. He noticed that even in the horrifying conditions of Auschwitz, many of the prisoners strove to do their work well. "The Italian bricklayer...hated Germans, their food, their language, their war; but when they set him to erect walls, he built them straight and solid, not out of obedience but out of professional dignity."[4] Like many prisoners, this man identified with his work, and to work badly would have betrayed who he was. In a sense, building a perfect wall for his German captors became an act of defiance, a way to affirm his identity and value, even if it was only to himself.

Any number of forms can provide people with a sense of identity: religion, nationality, marital status, political leanings, and so on. Even companies and regions can identify with forms. Think of Silicon Valley: the area has become so closely associated with the technology industry that more people know its nickname than the actual names of its cities.

Unification means being "at one" with the form, not just part of it, or represented by it, but fully absorbed in it. The most common example is being a man or woman. Bodies are forms, and being male or female so thoroughly affects our identity that it's nearly impossible to distinguish "who we are" from our gender.

THE RIGHT AMOUNT OF INVESTMENT

While identification and unification with form are good, you cannot choose to do them as you can choose to be involved or committed. The more significant degrees of investment come only with time and effort. No one level of investment is necessarily better than any other. Some forms are more deserving of our spirits, and often the degree to which we're invested will change. Any one member of an organization may *identify* with her work, may *commit* to the organization itself, and may get *involved* in a few extra activities here and there.

In general, the degree to which we invest in a form is equal to the amount of "resonance" we feel with it. The right form feeds spirit, and spirit in turn gives the form life. This is resonance—when there is a correspondence, an echo, between what a person does on the outside and who he or she is on the inside. Vitality depends on creating the conditions where this resonance can occur, where people want to invest their spirits into the organization's forms.

While there's no "right" degree of investment in any one form, organizations should strive to make their forms places where spirit finds resonance, and with which people will engage. The deeper people invest in an organization, the more of themselves they give. They work harder because they see the

> *There is no one best level of investment in form. Different forms demand and earn different levels of engagement.*

organization's success as their own. They're more loyal. They defend the organization's public image, and see themselves as ambassadors. Leaders at all levels need to make their forms appealing to spirit.

Bringing form and spirit together is a fundamental human need. A powerful form can shape and express the deepest parts of us; we can build our lives and organizations around a good form, and find both meaning and vitality. Uniting form and spirit and keeping them in sync is difficult, as we're about to see.

ENDNOTES

1. We owe credit for the idea of form and spirit in the world to Karl Rahner, the great German theologian. Though our work varies significantly from his, he provided us with a conceptual foundation on which to build.

2. May, Rollo. *The Courage to Create* (New York: Bantam Books, 1978), pg. 154.

3. Wright, Richard. "The Ethics of Living Jim Crow," *Uncle Tom's Children* (New York: HarperPerennial, 1993) pg. 15. Author's italics.

4. Levi, Primo. "A Conversation with Primo Levi by Philip Roth," from *Survival in Auschwitz* (New York: Collier Books, 1993), pg. 179.

II * Form and Spirit's Difficult Road

t would be wonderful if you could simply bring form and spirit together, then stand back and admire the energy. Unfortunately, even though vitality is powerful and can build on itself, it can still be damaged.

In this chapter, we describe some of the ways form and spirit can be separated. Specifically, we'll look at under-commitment, distrust, and failures of leadership. We will also begin to explore the biggest challenge of all: change.

The reason that these forces threaten vitality is that *they can separate form and spirit*.

CHALLENGE 1: UNDER-COMMITMENT

Many forms fail to elicit spirit. That isn't a bad thing. It would take too much energy to commit deeply to every form you encounter. Everyone needs to focus on the forms that matter most, but sometimes people withhold spirit even with important forms. We call this phenomenon *under-commitment*.

At one of our workshops, we met a man who refused to the point of absurdity to perform any task not in his job description. His cubicle was adjacent to the office laser printer, but if the printer ran out of paper, even if he were in the midst of printing something himself, he would not refill it. "It's not in my job description," he'd say, and call a secretary to do it for him, adding anywhere from several minutes to a half-hour to his project. His is an extreme example, but under-commitment is widespread in many organizations. The atmosphere in such organizations stifles spirit, and soon fewer and fewer people are willing to invest their energy and creativity.

> *MAJOR CHALLENGES TO VITALITY*
>
> *(Forces that can separate from and spirit)*
>
> *1. Under-commitment*
>
> *2. Distrust*
>
> *3. Poor leadership*
>
> *4. Change*

People who under-commit often have a good reason for it. Sometimes forms drive away spirit. Employees may have been burned by unkept promises, ongoing conflicts, too many demands on their time, or the feeling that even their most heroic efforts are unappreciated. For such people, under-commitment is just common sense. Is it any wonder the "light bulb" woman didn't bother to shine anymore?

> *In under-commitment, people fail to invest even in important forms.*

Sometimes under-commitment simply comes from the reticence of a person to commit. Often their reluctance has its source in old pain that was never resolved, or from a sense that they "deserve better," and they're waiting for something else to come along. Whether it's from cynicism, fear, arrogance, or some other reason, these people just don't want to engage spirit.

In any case, under-commitment threatens vitality because it *prevents the connection of form and spirit*. You can't have a successful team if your players refuse to join the game.

Under-Commitment and the Transactional Culture

Often, under-commitment is the *effect* of a conflict between form and spirit. When forms are hostile to spirit, under-commitment is the likely result.

Ironically, under-commitment also *causes* breaks between form and spirit. When enough people fail to invest spirit, a whole cynical culture arises. New members are initiated into this culture, as the "light bulb" woman was, by having their spirits dampened. The culture becomes self-sustaining: under-committers beat down any new, enthusiastic people, who in turn help beat down the next generation.

This happened in the government offices of a Minnesota county. The department was run by a director and an office manager who hated each other, so much that they wouldn't speak to each other. Their conflict ran so far back that no one knew how it had started. In the whole history of the department, there had never been a staff meeting because the two managers refused to share a room.

Both managers were incompetent in different ways. The director—totally passive and disinterested—gave his employees no guidance and never checked on the work they were doing. The office manager micro-managed with an iron fist. She verbally abused anyone who did anything she didn't like, and transferred anyone who challenged her to another department.

In such situations, people tend to become alienated, cynical, outraged, and/or depressed. They may feel objectified, like machine parts. Because they're treated like robots, they develop robotic behavior. They under-commit, put in their hours but not their hearts, and fixate on rules and become bureaucratic. In the worst cases, they protect themselves by turning selfish and turf-oriented, guarding their own territory, and refusing to reach out to other departments or individuals. They lose spontaneity and fail to take initiative. Just as the organization hurts them, their under-commitment hurts the organization.

> *Under-commitment* results from *and* causes *a conflict between form and spirit. An organization might be hostile to people's spirits, so they under-commit. In turn, their under-commitment hurts the organization.*

"Everybody comes to work, hunkers down in their own cubicle, and then goes home," one said. "We're so isolated it's like each of us is working in our own silo." New workers in particular were bewildered; they knew something was wrong, but nobody would tell them how things had gotten so bad. They quickly learned to keep their own heads down. Theirs was a *transactional culture*. We call it "transactional" because the business gets transacted, the basic tasks are accomplished, but it's all about form. There's no spirit and no vitality. It's like the principal who "stopped being the educational leader" of his school: he transacted business, but he left his spirit at home.

In transactional cultures, some people become so alienated and cynical that they begin to celebrate failure. An environmental organization's branch office was losing money and employees. The national headquarters sent in a team of trouble-shooters to infuse some expertise and enthusiasm into the office. The trouble-shooters found the place in a state of chaos, with no one who seemed interested in improving things. The trouble-shooters' optimism elicited only contempt, and their suggestions were met with scorn: "We've tried that already. It won't work."

> *A transactional culture is all form and no spirit. Business may get accomplished, but it's done with no spirit or vitality.*

After a week, one of the trouble-shooters broke down and wept in frustration. The office's director smiled in grim satisfaction. "These guys come in here and think they know how to fix things," he snarled. "We showed them." The culture of hostility toward spirit had become so entrenched that its members had actually begun to protect it.

Overcoming Under-Commitment

Under-commitment affects trust, change, and leadership. Distrust, poor leadership, and mismanaged change lead to under-commitment, and under-commitment leads to distrust, poor leadership, and mismanaged change.

Our main strategy for defeating under-commitment is to turn change, trust, and leadership into forces that augment vitality. If you manage change well, build trust, and lead with spirit, you can build forms that people will want to engage with. While under-commitment is a unique threat, you deal with it by dealing with the other threats we list below.

CHALLENGE 2: DISTRUST

The Auditors' Story

Not only can distrust damage vitality, it can make day-to-day business nearly impossible. All organizations depend on the trust of their customers and members, and losing that trust can destroy an organization. Recently, at least two enormous organizations—Enron and Andersen Accounting—were killed by their betrayals of public and investor trust.

In less spectacular breaches of faith, distrust damages organizations. At the bank where Martin and Grand worked, distrust was rampant. Not even the branch presidents trusted that they could speak their minds without derailing their careers. For the bank's auditors, the problem was worse.

The auditors were responsible for checking the books at newly acquired branch offices. It was a tough job and Grand knew that the auditors were exhausted. He asked us to host a three-day workshop for them at a nice resort.

The first day was a shocking contrast to what we'd seen among the top management. The branch presidents had hidden their problems, but among the auditors, the signs of burnout were everywhere. They slogged into the meeting with circles under their eyes, and a pall of cynical disinterest hung over the room. We tried to get them talking about their experiences, but all they would say is they were exhausted. Their energy was so depleted that we couldn't engage them in any meaningful conversation. We gave them the day off, telling them their first task was to relax, have fun, and rest.

The next morning, they arrived in better moods, and almost immediately opened up about what they were going through. The bank was changing rapidly, and like the presidents, they were having trouble adjusting to the new forms. Because of the speed of the changes, they felt enormous time pressure—they had to solve very complex problems rapidly. As a result, they put in long hours, making them more susceptible to mistakes, and increased the pressure they felt.

The more they talked, the more one crucial problem became obvious. One auditor put it like this: "I go into these branches, and my job is to check everything the staff has done. I'm the guy who comes in to bring down the hammer. I walk into those places and I can feel the hate in their eyes."

His story elicited murmurs of agreement and more stories like it. Virtually everyone in the room had been through the same thing, the sticky feeling of trying to do the job and being loathed for it. Their audits had been a regular part of doing business, a thorough double-check of the books, and now they felt as if they'd been set up as The Enemy. They felt distrusted, and this distrust turned their jobs into obstacle courses. Though they enjoyed auditing, the form of their jobs no longer offered any resonance. It wasn't rewarding their investment of spirit.

> *As people protect their spirits, distrust leads to under-commitment. It also turns daily business into an obstacle course.*

In order to nurture their spirits, they would have to find new forms. In a moment, we'll see how they did.

CHALLENGE 3: POOR LEADERSHIP

Four Ways Poor Leadership Can Damage Vitality

There are as many types of poor leadership as there are poor leaders. For simplicity's sake, we'll look at four basic ways leaders can damage vitality.

1. By mismanaging forms.

Leaders must be able to master forms (not just paperwork forms, but organizational structures) to be successful. When people talk about "poor leaders," they usually mean managers who don't know how to handle the forms around them. Maybe they don't keep up with essential paperwork, don't understand a manufacturing process, or can't fundraise or organize events. Maybe—as at

> *LEADERS CAN HINDER VITALITY IN AT LEAST FOUR WAYS:*
>
> *1. By mismanaging forms*
>
> *2. By attacking spirit*
>
> *3. By failing to commit spirit*
>
> *4. By neglecting spirit*

the bank—the forms are changing so rapidly that even competent managers can't keep up.

2. By attacking spirit.

Earlier we described the two leaders of a county office. One was a micromanaging tyrant who waged vendettas against any employee she didn't like. She attacked the office's spirit by squashing creativity and innovation, pitting employees against each other, and refusing to speak to the office's director. She poisoned the office spirit, creating an atmosphere in which only a fool would assert spontaneous leadership or proclaim a difference of opinion.

3. By failing to commit spirit.

The school principal failed as a leader for several years because he failed to commit spirit. He held the *form* of leadership (his title as principal), but he didn't have the *spirit* of a leader. He himself was not engaged, and his lack of engagement became a roadblock to others' engagement.

4. By neglecting spirit.

Some leaders don't recognize that spirit is out there. Maybe they don't have time for spirit, or don't know it even exists.

Tom Grand, the bank CEO, simply figured that because the bank's forms seemed to be successful (after all, the bank was growing exponentially), that its spirit was basically okay, though it might need a little boost. He wasn't attacking spirit, but he'd neglected to listen deeply to his people.

Reconnecting with Spirit

Much to Grand's credit, once people did start talking, he was willing to listen. More important, once he started listening, he knew he needed to pay closer attention to spirit, and knew he needed to give special attention to the burned-out auditors. We led their workshop at a resort, where they talked about feeling like The Enemy. It wasn't long before the auditors began to solve their problem.

The auditors agreed that whatever they did, they wanted to stop feeling like The Enemy. Could they build new forms that would both foster spirit and make the audits more effective? As soon as the question was asked, answers began to appear.

"For one thing," someone said, "we could help the staff understand how to do the paperwork." To standardize the bookkeeping, each bank branch had to complete stacks of paperwork. It was complicated work and the branch employees were given no training. Thinking about those employees' predicament, the auditors understood the resentment they had encountered a little better. It was as if they had handed each branch an exam it was bound to fail. What if the auditors set themselves up not as monitors, but as mentors? Ideas started pouring out. They could host workshops for the staff, set up hotlines to answer questions, and make themselves available for one-on-one tutoring. Suddenly, their spirits were engaged in the creation of new, better forms. They left the workshop with a plan to turn the auditing division into a clearinghouse for advice and information.

As the auditors engaged with this idea, markers of vitality started to appear. The auditors became more confident, recognized differences between themselves and other employees, and were able to make those differences an asset. They asserted spontaneous leadership and stewardship by developing initiatives to help their colleagues. Though they had reason to be defensive and to nurse their wounded egos, they took responsibility for their own mistakes and moved forward instead.

Over the next year or so, they were so successful that Grand asked many of them to lead team-building workshops for other departments. As the bank continued to expand, the auditors went from being burned out and despised to becoming catalysts of vitality.

CHALLENGE 4: CHANGE

The Profound Problem of Form

Forms are finite. They exist in particular places and times, which is how they set the limits that make them work. The fact that forms are finite is also their problem. For one thing, some forms are too limiting. The bank presidents' transactional meetings prevented them from talking about what really mattered. Forms like slavery and dictatorship assault spirit.

The most profound problem with form is that even the best forms won't last forever. They are guaranteed to end or change, and when they do, they separate from spirit. During times of change, vitality suffers because both form and spirit suffer. If an organization does not deal with changes in form *and* spirit, vitality can be extinguished altogether.

> *Forms are finite. They end, and when they do, spirit has to find new forms.*

Three Phases of Change

One way to define change is to say that it is *movement from one form to another.* Think of graduating from school and taking a job. You begin in one set of forms (taking classes and studying for exams) and you move to another set of forms (work hours, no summer vacation, getting a paycheck).

Change begins as one form ends (you graduate), and concludes when spirit becomes fully engaged in a new form (you adjust to your new job). Between these two forms comes a period of formlessness or chaos, when the old forms no longer work and the new ones aren't yet up and running. You might not find a job the minute you graduate, and spend a long time looking for a job (a new form) that suits your spirit. You might find a job, but it takes a while to adjust to the schedule and the new people.

> *THERE ARE* THREE PHASES OF CHANGE:
>
> *1. The end of the old form*
>
> *2. A period of formlessness or adjustment*
>
> *3. Investment in a new form*

Much of our understanding of this three-phase process comes from William Bridges, an expert on change and the author of many books, most notably *Transitions: Making Sense of Life's Changes* (Reading, MA: Addison-Wesley, 1980). We have re-interpreted his work (he does not use the terms form and spirit, for instance) to develop the following diagram (figure 2–1) of the three phases of change.

Figure 2–1

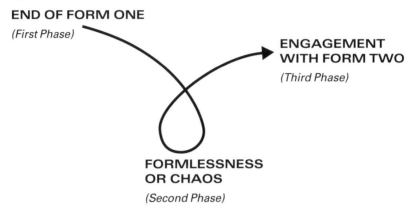

END OF FORM ONE
(First Phase)

**ENGAGEMENT
WITH FORM TWO**
(Third Phase)

**FORMLESSNESS
OR CHAOS**
(Second Phase)

The poet Richard Hugo, who piloted bombers in World War II, wrote that the war and its aftermath destroyed his "faith that change (I really mean loss) is paced slow enough for the blood to adjust."[1]

Hugo's equation of change with loss was very astute. Even when a change is "for the better," it almost always entails the loss of a form. This is what happens in phase one of change. The accounting procedures are discarded, the school is left behind. Any spirit that was tied to those forms collapses, too. Trust, comfort, a sense of order, and even identity can be torn apart when the old forms go.

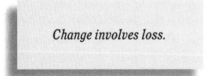

Change involves loss.

Once you've lost those things, chaos sets in. Chaos—the second phase of change—is a period of formlessness, when form and spirit are out of joint, like machine cogs that keep slipping out of alignment. Before you can engage in new forms, you have to pass through chaos and readjustment. This is especially true in traumatic change, such as when somebody dies or an organization shuts down.

Even when change isn't devastating, chaos can erupt when forms end. The bank presidents lost their old forms, and though they had new forms ready to go (like the accounting system), the period of adjustment was excruciating.

Chaos can be severe, or not so bad. Like at the bank, chaos is worse than it seems at first glance. Is there any way to predict the severity? Not precisely. The best indicator is the degree of investment in the forms being lost. The more engaged spirit is with the form, the deeper the sense of chaos, and the longer it's likely to last. If you don't care much about the form, you won't feel much loss or disorientation. Losing a crucial form—like a marriage, a home, or a job—can mean restructuring your life from the ground up.

Sometimes people never really get through the chaos. They get crushed by grief, rage, or confusion; they succumb to symptoms like alcoholism, over-work, or emotional isolation before they ever make it to the next form. One school principal needed eight years, a labor crisis, and our facilitation before he managed to put his spirit back into the school. An even more dramatic example is that of Queen Victoria. When her husband, Prince Albert, died, the queen ordered that his room be kept exactly as it had been during his life. She had her servants continue to bring his favorite breakfast to his room, as if he were still there.[2] In these cases, the loss becomes unfinished business—unresolved emotions and ideas—and the past becomes a ball and chain.

In order to survive chaos, it's important to know what you're up against. One crucial influence on chaos is that *change comes in two varieties*. "Random change" occurs when outside forces alter or destroy a form. "Developmental change" arises from internal pressure—when the spirit outgrows a form and needs to find a new one. The distinction is important because each kind of change causes a different kind of chaos.

RANDOM CHANGE

The presses were running normally one day at Brown Printing in Waseca, Minnesota, when the ceiling fell in. Two enormous rooftop air conditioning units suddenly plunged into the plant, smashing several machines and crushing two men. It happened so abruptly that no one understood what had happened for several minutes. Somehow, after several years, the air conditioners had simply become too heavy for the roof beams.

The men were dead. Both had young families, and in this small plant in a small town, everyone knew them. Everybody was horrified. The company president, torn apart himself, asked us to help people cope with the tragedy. We talked to groups of employees in the cafeteria and spoke to individuals in private. They were grief-stricken, appalled, and scared. One man said he kept being awakened in the middle of the night by nightmares of his ceiling collapsing. He'd even climbed onto the roof once to reassure himself there was nothing up there to fall on him.

> *Random change happens to people and is caused by sudden outside events.*

What they'd all experienced was a particularly brutal random change. Random change occurs when something unexpected happens to a form. Random change happens *to* people; they don't control it. Another obvious example is the attacks of September 11, which destroyed countless forms—not to mention lives.

There can be good random changes as well as bad. You win the lottery. You get an unexpected raise or promotion. By chance, you meet the person who will become the love of your life.

Change can be difficult because when spirit is invested in a form, losing it is painful. That's especially true during random change, in which a form ends before the spirit is ready to let go, as in this Calvin and Hobbes cartoon[3] (figure 2–2).

Figure 2–2

CALVIN AND HOBBES © 1987 Watterson. Reprinted with permission of UNIVERSAL PRESS SYNDICATE. All rights reserved.

This cartoon beautifully illustrates a common effect of random change: the feeling that the spirit is still attached to a form that no longer exists. Calvin's feeling that the raccoon is still alive inside him indicates that his spirit is still engaged in his relationship with it, yet the form is no longer there to reward this engagement. There's no longer resonance between his inner and outer worlds, which is painful.

When the old form disappears, the spirit is left in a paradoxical situation. It is still invested in the form, but the form is gone. You still love the person who's died or walked out, you still identify with the job you just lost, you still depend on the departed leader. Even in a good change, losing old forms can be disorienting. The experience of random change is like that of people who lose an arm or leg but can still "feel" it there. They may itch, but there's nothing to scratch.

In a random change, the form ends and the spirit plunges into chaos (figure 2–3). Shock and panic may paralyze a person or even an entire organization. Looking to the future may seem impossible, at least for a while. If you've lost an identifying form, moving ahead means developing a new identity—becoming a "new" person or organization.

Moving ahead too quickly, moreover, often feels like a betrayal of the old form. When somebody dies, loved ones may not *want* to get over the grief, because it feels like they're betraying the person. The same is true when close colleagues are laid off. Some employees who survive job cuts believe they have an ethical responsibility to hold a grudge on behalf of co-workers who are no longer there.

Figure 2–3

RANDOM CHANGE

During random change, a form ends or is seriously altered, leaving spirit isolated. Until the spirit is ready to find another form, it experiences an often-traumatic period of chaos and formlessness.

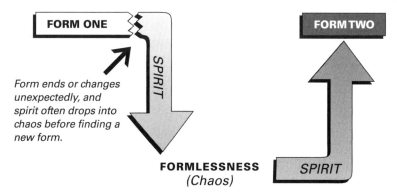

While the shock of random change causes pain by itself, the real danger comes in the way people handle the loss. People undergoing random change may feel dread, anxiety, even despair. Will anything ever be the same? How will I cope? They need time and help to recover from significant loss. Otherwise they may be burdened with "unfinished business" and get caught in the past.

> *Letting go of an old form sometimes feels like a betrayal.*

In the next chapter and in our discussion of Clarification in Part Two, we describe ways of coping with the shock and chaos of change. It's true that you never really get over some losses, and we don't believe that a devastating loss is ever "for the best." But even the most difficult change can become an opportunity for growth. People and organizations can incorporate loss into their lives and go on. Random change can become developmental change.

DEVELOPMENTAL CHANGE

Unlike the disaster at Brown Printing, the changes at the bank and at Gordon Burns' agricultural firm were not random. They were *developmental*: planned, strategic efforts to get to the "next level." The bank had outgrown its old accounting procedures. With a dozen new branches, it needed to find ways to centralize its data. Rather than being surprised by the loss of forms, the bankers had deliberately left their old forms behind.

> *In a developmental change, the spirit outgrows existing forms and needs to find new ones.*

Developmental change is inevitable. Even perfect forms are perfect only because they meet current needs. A uterus is the perfect place for a fetus, with the nutrients and protection the baby needs to develop, but that very perfection causes a "problem": the baby does develop. After nine months, the uterus becomes too restrictive, and if the child isn't born, it will die. Mother and baby must find a new form. Every individual and organization goes through such developmental phases. They must escape from old forms like a snake shedding its skin.

Periods of developmental change (figure 2–4) usually begin with the realization that old forms are no longer working. These forms don't reward or express spirit as they once did. Spirit begins to look for something better. For Gordon Burns, this meant abolishing the traditional, outdated boundaries between his agricultural research divisions. For the bank, rapid growth meant that the old accounting and loan procedures no longer worked.

Figure 2–4

DEVELOPMENTAL CHANGE

Developmental change begins when a form outlives its usefulness. Spirit leaves it behind to look for new forms. Sometimes it is clear what the new forms will be, often it is not. In either case, spirit passes through a swamp of formlessness as it lets go of the old form and acclimates to the new.

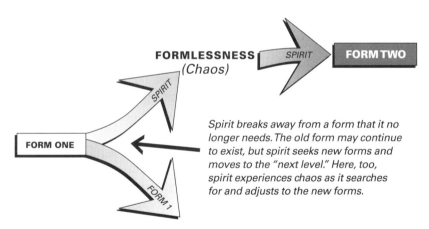

FORMLESSNESS *(Chaos)*

SPIRIT → **FORM TWO**

FORM ONE

Spirit breaks away from a form that it no longer needs. The old form may continue to exist, but spirit seeks new forms and moves to the "next level." Here, too, spirit experiences chaos as it searches for and adjusts to the new forms.

Of course, changing Burns' company and the bank weren't simple. Employees were confused and anxious. They were engaged in the old forms, and now they had to give them up. Even if the new forms were easy to install and understand, people would have to let go of their habits and engage with unfamiliar forms. As it happened, the new forms were complicated and difficult to install, which made the transitions even tougher. This is why even "good" changes prove to be so difficult.

Ultimately, though, these *were* good changes. Burns' realignment and the bank's new procedures allowed both organizations to grow. Because the executives had listened to their people's problems, questions, and objections, the organizations' forms and spirits became stronger. Each institution moved to the next level, which is why we refer to the changes as developmental.

THE BLURRY LINE BETWEEN RANDOM AND DEVELOPMENTAL CHANGE

The distinction between random and developmental change is an important one, but the line between them isn't always clear. Different people may experience the same event in radically different ways. Gordon Burns saw the changes he wanted to make as developmental. He wanted to move the company to the next level. For many of the scientists the change came at random, dropped on them by a man they barely knew.

This often happens at organizations—developmental change for some is random for others. For instance, managers have greater access to information than the rank and file. As a result, they may make decisions that are clearly in the company's long term interest, but to employees who get the news after the change is already underway, the decision may seem capricious. The surprise can cut both ways, as when angry employees shock their supervisors by quitting in droves or organizing a union.

Some changes are partly random and partly development, and one type of change can turn into the other.

Not only can different people see a change in different ways, developmental change can become random, and vice versa. At the bank and the research firm, the developmental changes nearly spun out of control and became random. If they hadn't found ways to solve their problems, the institutions could have floated adrift, at the mercy of whatever random events hit them.

FROM RANDOM TO DEVELOPMENTAL: THE SUBURBAN CHURCH'S STORY

Random change can also become an opportunity for development. This happened at a large suburban church. Its talented, charismatic pastor had built the church up over several years, turning it into a player on the local and national scenes. The pastor worked so hard that he burned out. He abruptly announced that he needed to take a leave of absence. A few months later he told the congregation that he wouldn't be back at all. For the people who loved and relied on him, it was a stunning, random change. (The departure of a leader is among the most common random changes.)

Fortunately, the church board named a terrific interim pastor who understood the need to address the "spirit" side of the change. He began with workshops for the church staff, who felt the impact most strongly. We facilitated a dialogue in which staff members talked about the meaning of the loss, and where the church had been and where they wanted it to go. As they talked, they noted that until now they'd never assessed their own work as a staff. They had rarely reflected on their role in the church. The main reason was that they considered themselves transitory. None had a sense that the jobs were long-term. The congregation was made up of busy professionals who often moved for job opportunities; church staffers came and went at a rapid rate. When the group tallied its own turnover, they realized that on a staff of about a dozen, 19 people had come and gone within recent memory. Nobody had acknowledged all these arrivals and departures. They hardly bade farewell to those who left, and never really welcomed newcomers. The resignation of the pastor, who had anchored the church through all this turnover, only augmented the feeling of impermanence. Losing the pastor made the staff realize how many other people they had lost.

To help resolve this unfinished business, the staff held a half-day ceremony in which they set up nineteen tables in a church conference room, one table for each person who left. The staff members went from table to table. If they had known the person represented by a given table, they sat down and wrote a letter of farewell. If the letter was positive, they mailed it to the person. If it raised old conflicts, they sealed it in an envelope and, after a special liturgy, burned it.

The ceremony helped the staff put the past behind them. Then, ready to move on, they declared a "Month of Transition." They cleared their desks of any work that wasn't essential and focused the church on the future. They interviewed every family in the congregation, asking them to evaluate the parish's past performance, make suggestions, and share their visions of what they wanted the church to become and what they wanted in a new pastor. They asked whether people were interested in volunteering (thereby opening opportunities for stewardship and spontaneous leadership).

Finally, with all this information at hand, they knew what kind of pastor the congregation wanted and what they wanted him or her to do. They also had engaged the congregation in the process, giving people a voice in the decision. Not surprisingly, the pastor they brought in was a crackerjack who built on the church's success. He implemented many of the recommendations that congregants had made, expanded the church's programs with initiatives of his own, and stabilized the staff. In this way, the church turned a random change into a developmental one, moving itself to the next level.

THE CRUCIAL QUESTION OF CHANGE

Change has serious implications for vitality. It separates spirit from form, and usually leads to some degree of chaos. We live in a time when change is omnipresent; it is essential. Sometimes it drizzles on us mildly but steadily, other times it washes everything away in great floods. *If vitality comes from the interaction of form and spirit, but change separates form and spirit, how do you maintain vitality in today's rainforest of continuous change?* This question is at the crux of vitality.

Organizations can take steps to keep people engaged on a number of levels. For one thing, they can engage people in the process of change itself by delegating responsibilities and devolving decision-making power.

They can create *interim forms* (see chapter four, "Inside Change") to provide stability during periods of flux. They can use Clarification to understand exactly what the changes mean to individuals (see chapters four and five, "Finding a New Form"). They can build trust among their members, because when forms are falling apart around them, all people have is each other (see chapter six, "Trust"). They can encourage leadership and creativity in all their people, so that leaders step forward and point the way toward new visions and new forms (see chapter seven). Together, these steps can turn chaos into transformative energy.

SUMMARY

The past two chapters have explained the ways form and spirit interact and how they create vitality. When an organization's structures and policies are both effective and welcoming of spirit, people will engage with the organization. They will feel some resonance between their work and who they are. They will know they can make a difference. Spirit and form generate enormous vitality when they mesh.

Unfortunately, there are significant threats to an organization's vitality. Under-commitment, distrust, and poor leadership can prevent spirit from meshing with form. Change, which by its very nature separates form and spirit, is pandemic. Sustaining vitality in the face of these challenges is the task of every organization. The stakes are high because to fail is to risk catastrophe.

ENDNOTES

1. Hugo, Richard. "Letter to Matthews from Barton Street Flats," *Selected Poems* (New York: WW Norton & Co., 1979) pg. 143.

2. Schama, Simon. "Balmorality," *The New Yorker*, August 11, 1997.

3. Watterson, Bill. *Something Under the Bed is Drooling: A Calvin and Hobbes Collection* (Kansas City: Andrews and McMeel, 1988), pg. 95.

III ✳ Three Principles
of Vitality

THE UNIVERSITY'S STORY

n the late 1960s, Chuck took a job as a professor at a college in Minnesota. After a few years, he was promoted to Assistant Vice President. The college was performing exceptionally well. This public school had traditionally served students from the local town and surrounding region, but recently began to draw from across the Midwest. Enrollments and new programs went way up. The school couldn't hire faculty fast enough. The state changed the school's designation from college to university—a big boost to its prestige—and construction of a new, modern campus quickened. The effects of this growth would soon spark a dramatic crisis, and the university's vitality would be seriously threatened.

The university's crisis quickly became a personal crisis for Chuck (and our whole family). This was one of our most excruciating work experiences, but it taught us lessons we use to this day. Most important, we distilled Three Principles of Vitality from the experience. These principles identify the hidden dynamics of form and spirit, and they describe the psychological effects of change. They explain what went wrong at the university, as well as at Grand's bank, the school with the disengaged principal, and Gordon Burns' agricultural company. More important, these three principles point the way through such crises. They offer a blueprint for vitality. We'll introduce the principles here, then later examine each one in detail.

During the period that the university was growing so rapidly, students were staging demonstrations against the war in Vietnam. One in particular, a huge march, frightened many members of the community with its vehemence. People feared that the university was out of control. It wasn't long before enrollments stalled, then declined. Some students dropped out. At the same time, the pool of graduating high school seniors began to shrink. The students who dropped out weren't going to be replaced. Within a couple of years, the administration had to reduce the faculty by thirty positions.

All this occurred before participatory decision-making had become widespread. Chuck's boss, the Vice President for Academic Affairs, simply began combing through each department's roster, looking for jobs to cut. Fortunately, a number of faculty positions were empty. He cut them all. It seemed like a good idea, because though the jobs were eliminated, nobody was laid off.

The faculty, however, were furious. They felt they should have been consulted on such an important matter, and convened a special session of the faculty senate to consider censuring the administration. They summoned Chuck's boss to appear before the senate to justify his decision. He couldn't make it and Chuck had to take his place. He found himself alone in front of a room full of professors, trying to defuse their anger.

Only a few months earlier, Chuck had been a professor himself. He had little experience in upper-level administration, and considered the faculty members as friends and colleagues. At the meeting he tried to persuade them that although the cuts had been made without their consent, it was all for the best. No one lost a job—only positions, not people, had been cut. The faculty didn't buy it. They saw him and the whole administration as paternalistic, acting as if they had all the right answers. They voted to censure the administration for its "callous disregard of faculty input."

Chuck took the censure personally. He felt he failed both the administration and the faculty, and worried that his colleagues' anger might never subside. On one level, he could understand the censure. The faculty was frightened for their jobs; they felt powerless and angry, but the censure only seemed to add to the chaos. Some students and their parents, already worried about the demonstrations, began to wonder whether the college was in good hands. Only two years earlier, the college had been a success. Now it looked as if its new buildings would remain half-filled. The old forms had collapsed, and the school was immersed in chaos, desperately in need of new forms. Its former vitality was nowhere to be found.

Chuck was promoted to interim Vice President the following year, as enrollment continued to decline. The drop-off was so steep that one of Chuck's first tasks was to eliminate eighty jobs, a whopping twenty-five percent of the faculty. He was terrified. The school had already eliminated every vacant position; unlike the previous year, these cuts wouldn't just be on paper. He had to lay off *people*, some of whom were his friends. Worse yet, because he had to cut non-tenured faculty, he'd have to lay off some of the school's most talented young teachers—the very people who taught the largest classes and who generated the bulk of the college's tuition income. Losing that income would probably necessitate even more cuts. Eliminating those eighty jobs felt like drinking poison in preparation for jumping off a cliff.

Chuck wasn't sure how to proceed, but he realized that he couldn't make any final decisions by himself. The year before, the cuts had seemed relatively easy to decide on, but chaos had erupted. This year, the cuts would be even more controversial. He couldn't just sit in his office and send out pink slips; the place would explode.

As he considered his dilemma, Chuck suddenly understood a deceptively simple truth: *significant events cause reactions*. When something significant happens to an important form, people react. They may be sad, angry, or exultant, but if their spirit was invested in the form, they will react to change. He was stunned by this simple lesson. He and his boss had never *imagined* that the faculty would care about position cuts as long as no person lost a job. At the censure meeting, Chuck had dismissed faculty concerns about an important event that had a direct impact on their lives. He had neglected their spirits. No wonder they had been angry. What's more, the faculty had suspected more cuts would be coming, and next time they might lose their jobs. Why shouldn't they want to at least *discuss* the cuts, if only to feel they had some input into their own destiny?

As we continue to work with organizations, this simple but fundamental truth—significant events generate reactions—has become our *first principle of vitality*.

The same concept translates into the language of form and spirit. When someone invests spirit into a form, any change to the form affects the spirit. As the bank presidents discovered, even "good" events can throw an organization into a period of formlessness, and the more important the form, the more dramatic people's reaction to changing it.

> *First principle of vitality:*
> **Significant events trigger reaction.**

How could Chuck do a better job this time? The university seemed to have two tasks before it. One was to figure out how to stop the slide in enrollment; the other, cut those eighty jobs. After a lot of thought and consultation with colleagues, Chuck came up with a plan.

The reason for the college's tailspin had seemed clear: the student demonstrations had alienated nearly everyone in sight. More than that, there was the undeniable fact the school had undergone massive changes—a spectacular expansion followed by a sudden enrollment collapse—and these changes had affected every corner of the university. In order to figure out what happened, what those events meant, and how they'd affected people, Chuck and the other administrators sponsored a series of "speaking circles," to which anyone with an interest in the college was invited. The main questions to address were, "How did the school get to this point?" and "How do we turn things around?" The primary rule: "Be honest."

Lots of people showed up, students, parents, university faculty and staff, and townspeople. They had many complaints. One thing became evident right away—the demonstrations were not the only concern. Even when the college had seemed to be thriving, there had been hidden problems. Student orientation didn't even exist, people said, and student advising was haphazard. The school gave little guidance to freshmen or undecided majors and didn't involve parents. As the university had expanded, students had found themselves more alone, with few resources for sorting out their options. Townspeople complained about the demonstrations and rowdy student parties—but they complained even more that the college ignored their complaints. For a while, the meetings seemed chaotic, but after a while, a pattern emerged from the discussions: the school had become complacent and was neglecting its students. It wasn't meeting its responsibilities to the community or to its own employees. The school had become so impressed with itself and so ambitious that it failed in its most basic duties. The result: people were upset and confused; they were avoiding or quitting the college. They were, in short, disengaging.

This was our first professional lesson in what would later become our *second principle of vitality*: Ignoring people's reactions does not make those reactions go away. Instead, the reactions lurk in the shadows and continue to affect your organization.

Life at the college, as at Grand's bank, seemed outwardly "good." The school had been expanding and was financially successful. Yet in both cases, management paid attention only to what was happening to the forms. They neglected spirit, allowing confusion and animosity to fester.

Second principle of vitality: **Those reactions do not go away. Ignore them and they go "underground" and continue to influence the organization.**

In the years since the university's crisis, we've seen this principle played out dozens of times. We once worked with a corporation that was downsizing. For its entire history, the company had been known for its loyalty to its employees. These were its first large-scale lay-offs.

In announcing the downsizing, one division supervisor called his employees together and announced, "In three months, a third of you will be laid off. We don't know who it will be yet, and we won't identify anybody until the day it happens." He didn't even wait for the news to sink in before he warned them, "Now, I want you all to come to work tomorrow with a smile on your faces."

Most bosses don't stomp on their employees' reactions quite so egregiously. Many don't need to: the organizational culture in many places is so hostile to spirit that everyone just swallows their reactions because it's not safe to have any.

The reactions don't disappear. A few years ago, people thought you could just throw garbage "away." Now we know that "away" is somewhere, often a landfill, and even though the garbage is buried, it will eventually leak into groundwater. That's what happened at this company. People did smile for the boss as if everything was okay, but their enthusiasm vanished. Even those who survived the lay-offs distrusted the company and no longer gave their best effort. They loathed their boss, who had avoided open conflict and who became largely ineffective.

The university administrators had stepped on people's reactions, too.

They didn't listened to faculty fears or input, they neglected community relations. With the "speaking circles," they were now listening. As people's reactions came into the open, the school could identify and begin to solve its deep-seated problems. It began by rewriting its mission statement. The new mission affirmed that the college was a regional institution—not a national one, as it had once aspired to be—and its primary obligation was to its students. The statement was a realistic vision for its future. New forms were built to make this vision a reality. Every sector of the university developed new systems to help students. New recruiting, orientation, and counseling systems were created, along with a community relations office.

With the university re-oriented toward a new, clear mission, a committee of administrators, students, faculty, staff, and alumni set about to determine criteria for the eighty job cuts. The task was still a tough one, but now was being made by people who had a stake in the decision. Just as important, the decisions were being made in the context of a clear new mission and realistic priorities.

When the lay-off plan was finalized, the faculty senate praised the administration for "the thorough, humane, and participatory manner in which the cuts were made." In the following years, the school's enrollment remained constant in spite of continually decreasing numbers of college-age students.

Third principle of vitality: **Dealing openly with reactions can create opportunities for growth and revitalization— even in the most difficult circumstances.**

We learned a lot from this experience. We've discovered elementary business principles, such as "serve your customer." What's really interesting is this paradox: In the first year, thirty positions with nobody in them were cut, and conflict erupted. In the second year, eighty people lost their jobs, but the faculty senate praised the administration, and the university was revitalized. What made the difference? Clearly, the most significant factor during the second round of cuts, was that the administration let people participate in the process. People had some input into their destiny. Even those who lost their jobs, though they were upset, agreed that the process had been fair. The lesson we learned has become our third principle of vitality: *If people can work through their reactions, even the most difficult situations become opportunities for growth and development.*

Together, these three principles lead to a crucial conclusion: *when it comes to maintaining vitality, what is decisive is not* what *happens, but* how *we deal with it.* Outwardly good events can have catastrophic consequences, while painful ones can lead to renewal. It depends on how organizations and their people respond.

Too often, organizations deal with events *transactionally* — something that happens only to forms and not to spirit. This is why many management fads fail. Ideally, a program like Total Quality Management should lead to a shift in mindset—the business utilizing it should emerge with a flattened

> **What matters most to vitality is not *what happens*, but *how one responds.***

hierarchy, an emphasis on teams, and forums for creative thinking. But many organizations only adopt its outer trappings, such as the lingo and the meeting guidelines. When it came to actually getting managers to relinquish some control to their team, or getting employees to venture crazy and creative ideas, many efforts fell flat. This is what happened at the university. The first year, the problems had all been handled transactionally. No one ever discussed the source of the problem. There was no forum for people to discuss their reactions. (On the contrary, the administrators didn't even imagine that people would *have* reactions).

> *The opposite of a transactional culture is a* **reflective culture.**

The alternative to transaction is *reflection*. In the second year, the university reflected on the causes and meaning of what was happening. When it did, its very core was transformed: the university became a community. Its entire mission changed, giving everyone a new understanding of his or her role. People's spirits got back on board.

The rest of this chapter describes the three principles of vitality in detail and gives practical tips for dealing with them. Even more important, we provide the foundation for later discussions of the Clarification process and the issues raised by change, trust, and leadership. To recap, the three principles are:

1. Significant events cause reactions.
2. Those reactions may be ignored or suppressed, but they do not go away. They can cause lingering problems and resistance to any new forms.
3. Paying attention to those reactions make it possible for an organization to turn difficult situations into opportunities for growth and development.

These principles teach us that for vitality the important thing is not *what* happens to an organization, but *how* it responds. The *reflective organization* is one that pays attention to and learns from people's reactions to events.

THE FIRST PRINCIPLE OF VITALITY

Significant events cause reactions

Event and Experience

When we facilitate workshops, one of the first things we talk about is the difference between *events* and *experience*. "Events" are facts, things that happen. For instance, a company moves its headquarters or develops a new product line. "Experience" is how people react to events—their intellectual and emotional responses. Experience tells us the *meaning* of an event. Events happen to form, experience happens to spirit.

Events and experiences are what happen to form and spirit *over time*. Events *change* forms, and experience is the spirit's reaction. For example, think of the form of a grocery store. Over time, the store gets run down and dirty—that's an event. Customers begin to find shopping there distasteful—

that's an experience; it's what happens to their spirit in response to the event. The store owners overhaul the place—another event. Shoppers get excited about returning to it—an experience.

At Tom Grand's bank, there were a number of events: the acquisition of new branches, the shift to new accounting and loan procedures, and the establishment of new meeting formats. There were many experiences: Martin's feeling that he was "covered in blood," the auditors' burnout, and Grand's dismay when he discovered that beneath the surface, the changes he initiated weren't all ice cream and roses.

> *Events and experiences are what happen to form and spirit* **over time.** *Events happen to form, experience is the spirit's reaction.*

People's experience of the events had as much an impact on the bank as the events themselves, but for a long time these experiences remained hidden. They were like black holes, invisibly exerting gravity on everything the bank attempted. As long as the bankers worked *transactionally*, talking about form only, these important experiences would remain hidden.

Sometimes people don't talk about experience because they assume everyone's sharing the same experience. It's impossible to predict everyone's reactions to events. We were facilitating a workshop at a large corporation when the company announced it would spin off a major division. Everyone was shocked. Beyond the surprise, there were as many reactions to the spin-off as there were people. Some were scared, others angry, and others thrilled at the new opportunities. You can never assume that all people will react to events in a predictable, consistent way.

Flow

Events and experiences come in tandem. When an event changes an important form, it causes experience. Experiences, in turn, influence events. A lot of energy flows from events to experience and back again. To make this energy work for your organization, you want to encourage this flow.

At the university, the *event* of the first round of layoffs sparked the *experience* of anxiety and rage, as shown in figure 3–1:

Figure 3–1

EVENT
(layoffs)

EXPERIENCE
(anger, fear)

That's not all that happened. The faculty's *experience* (their anger and fear) led to a second *event*: the censure. So the "inside" of the process began to impact the "outside." In this way, energy flows not only from event to experience, but also back again (figure 3–2).

Figure 3–2

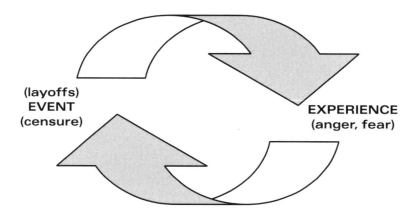

(layoffs)
EVENT
(censure)

EXPERIENCE
(anger, fear)

Notice that this interchange is identical to that of form and spirit. This process continues with each event and experience influencing the other in turn. At the university, the "dialogue" between event and experience looked like this (figure 3–3):

Figure 3–3

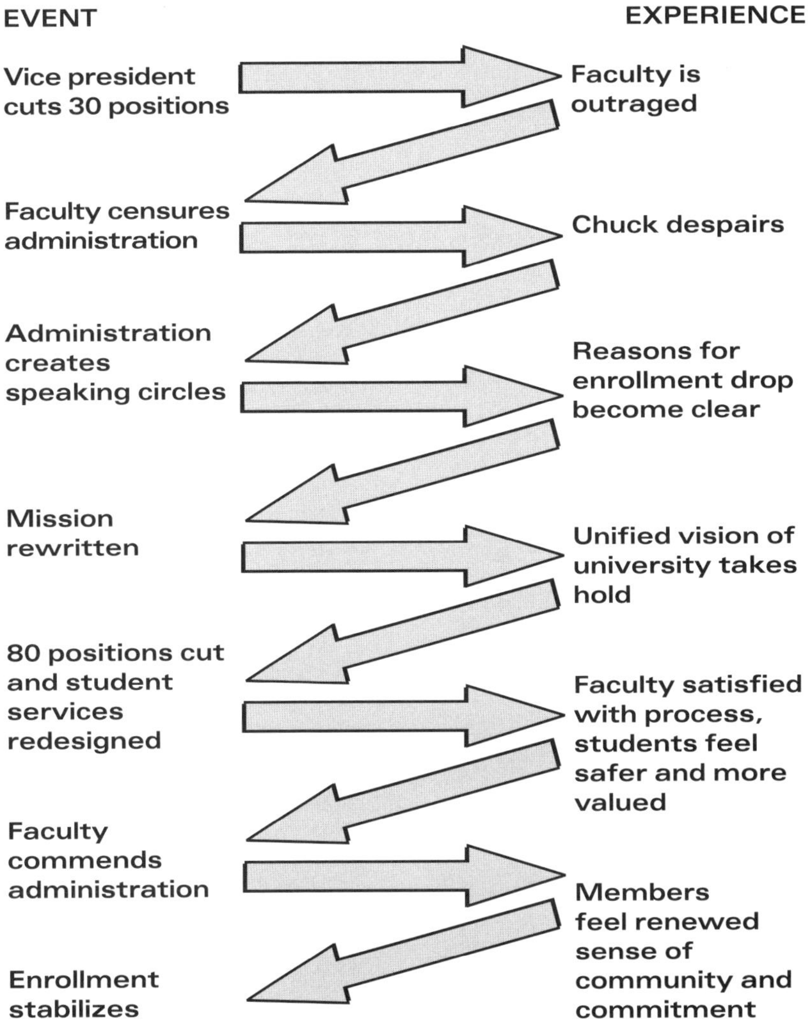

EVENT   **EXPERIENCE**

Vice president cuts 30 positions → Faculty is outraged

Faculty censures administration → Chuck despairs

Administration creates speaking circles → Reasons for enrollment drop become clear

Mission rewritten → Unified vision of university takes hold

80 positions cut and student services redesigned → Faculty satisfied with process, students feel safer and more valued

Faculty commends administration → Members feel renewed sense of community and commitment

Enrollment stabilizes

The faculty censure (an event) created bad feelings in Chuck (an experience), who initiated a new process for making the cuts (another event), which elicited ideas and feelings (experience) from the entire university community, which led to the revision of the university's mission (an event), and so on.

When this process began, people believed the administration did not care about them and was arbitrarily deciding their destiny. The university began to adapt its forms (by creating the speaking circles) so that people had an *opportunity* to become engaged. People bought into the process and participated. The university responded to their ideas, changing still more forms (its mission, the structure of the retention programs). This proved the school was trustworthy, which encouraged and allowed the community to feel even more engaged. People responded by investing spirit even more deeply.

Figure 3–4

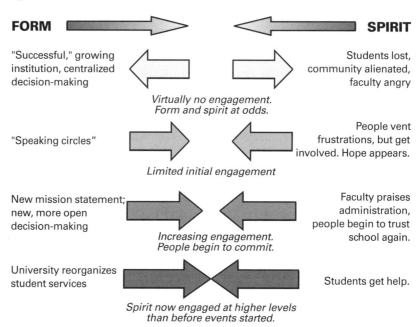

As this process went on, form and spirit grew closer together (figure 3–4). In the beginning, events like the initial thirty cuts and the faculty censure alienated spirit. Later events were in sync with spirit, and even though the later cuts were more severe, they didn't damage vitality like the earlier cuts. Despite the difficult events, people had become engaged again. This flow between form and spirit is vitality. The flow of vitality arises when an organization is reflective rather than transactional, when it pays attention to people's reactions and experiences. If it doesn't, those reactions grow like untreated cancers.

THE SECOND PRINCIPLE OF VITALITY

Reactions to events do not disappear by themselves. If ignored or suppressed, they hang around as "unfinished business" which continue to damage vitality. They may even show up as symptoms that seem unrelated to the original event.

Dams in the Current

The first step toward vitality is getting the flow moving between event and experience, as previously diagrammed. Conversely, the quickest way to drain vitality is to block this flow, and that's too easy to do.

Any high school student knows that in public, you express honest opinions at your peril. The demands of adolescent conformity, of not rocking the boat, are immense; for many kids, speaking about the bewilderment of growing up is simply not a risk worth taking. For many adults, the situation is the same. At the bank, only Martin, who was a president and close to retirement, felt secure enough to speak honestly.

There are all kinds of reasons for people in organizations not to talk about their experience. These reasons fall into two categories: active suppression and neglect. Organizations either actively discourage people from speaking up or simply fail to listen.

> *TWO WAYS TO BLOCK THE FLOW*
>
> Suppression
>
> Neglect

Active Suppression of Experience

An example of active suppression is the supervisor who ordered his staff to "come to work tomorrow with a smile" when a third of them were about to be laid off. He left no doubt that his employees' reactions were not wanted.

By contrast, consider the actions of Steve Palmquist, owner of a small oil wholesale business and gas station. After twenty years, he decided to sell part of his wholesale business in order to concentrate on other ventures. Doing so meant several of his employees would have a new boss. To announce the sale, he called each employee into his office privately to explain what he was doing and why. Then he took a crucial extra step. He told each person that his decision would stick—there was no turning back—but he wanted to give them the opportunity to tell him what they thought. "If you want to yell at me, that's fine," he said. "If you've got questions, I'll try to answer them. I'd also like you to take the rest of the day off, talk to your family or whoever you want to, sleep on it, and come back and talk to me again tomorrow." He allowed them to have a reaction, and gave them a safe place to express it.

The difference between the two men is clear: one was open to his people's experience, the other tried to suppress it. Active suppression doesn't always need to be stated explicitly. Many organizations send unspoken messages by firing or refusing to promote anyone who speaks up.

You can even suppress yourself. All of us do this occasionally, when speaking up would be inappropriate or counter-productive, we tell ourselves to keep quiet. This can become a problem when we consistently fail to say what's on our minds.

Sometimes suppressers may not be consciously aware of what they're doing. At one computer firm, decentralized decision-making was all the rage. The CEO, who'd built the business from a small firm to one with hundreds of employees, had always made every important decision by himself. Now he excitedly talked about empowering employees. He also wanted to hand off major decisions to a management team, and wanted input from people who would be affected.

The problem was that he didn't actually let anyone else contribute to a decision. Squads of employees researched their options carefully, and would develop recommendations with the management team. More often than not, the CEO disregarded their advice and made a different decision. He could never explain exactly how he'd decided. It just "felt right" to him.

His top executives—not to mention the employees themselves—became increasingly frustrated. Finally, five of his top managers confronted him in a meeting. They were honest and forceful. "We don't have a team here," one said, "because we don't know how decisions are made or understand our goals." Another added, "I don't even know if I'm actually *on* this team. I know I'm invited to the meetings, but no one's ever told me I'm part of the team, and you certainly don't treat me like a team member." In statements that echoed the bankers' complaints, they said that no one brought up substantive issues in meetings because the meetings were a waste of time. All the real decisions were made afterward, in the CEO's office.

For a long time, the five executives levied their criticisms, citing examples and describing the intellectual and emotional consequences of trying so hard to swim against the current. With just a few minutes remaining in the meeting, the CEO responded by giving a pep talk.

The problems the team was complaining about, he said, didn't really exist. Things weren't so bad. The team needed to think more optimistically. Then time was up; the CEO gathered his papers and left.

It was an amazing performance. Unlike Grand, who'd tried hard to understand his people and who took their criticisms to heart, this CEO totally ignored his team. Most perplexing of all was the chasm between the CEO's stated desire to share power and his complete refusal to actually do so. It seemed he honestly had no idea of the damage he was inflicting.

The management team left in despair.

Neglect of Experience

In active suppression, leaders tell people their experience doesn't matter. Neglect occurs when those who *could* ask about people's experience, don't. As one executive told us, "I must confess that in 25 years as a president and CEO, the thought never occurred to me to ask how people might react to my orders and decisions." An article in the *Harvard Business Review* tells a similar story about Harry Denton, the CEO of Delarks department stores. He managed to turn around the stock price of the ailing company, but he did so largely through massive layoffs for which he gave no warning. "His view," says the author, "was that when a company is in deep financial trouble and a new CEO is brought in to save it, *everyone knows that layoffs are next*"[1] (italics added). He assumed not only that everyone knew layoffs were coming, but that because they knew, their *experience* of it didn't matter.

A common excuse for neglect is that *there's not enough time to pay attention to people's reactions*. Especially in business, where competition continuously pushes the pace, managers often feel that while it might be nice to provide forums for their employees' reactions, there's simply no time. (We would reply that there's no time *not* to deal with reactions.)

This is not to say that managers who neglect experience are "bad." Many organizations have focused for so long on quantifiable data that few people really know *how* to address qualitative experience. Leaders anywhere may have justifiable fears about opening up a forum where people may be critical of them or ask unanswerable questions. Employees may not want to talk, even if given the chance, because they're scared, or not participating gives them a sense of control, or they aren't sure how to proceed. Part Two, "Clarification," suggests a number of ways to overcome these obstacles.

> *Many organizations have focused for so long on quantifiable data that they don't know how to learn from qualitative experience.*

Neglect isn't always the fault of management. We've worked with a number of organizations where the leadership was eager to open dialogue, but the rank and file was not. This happens often in school districts, universities, and other organizations where there is an entrenched or tenured old guard. The veterans may have good reason to distrust management, having fought furious labor battles or survived purges, but their battle scars and secure positions often make them impervious to any suggestion they could work cooperatively (or speak openly) with administrators.

Whether it's from neglect or active suppression, the failure to attend to people's reaction blocks the flow between event and experience. On the following chart, the blockage looks like this (figure 3–5):

Figure 3–5

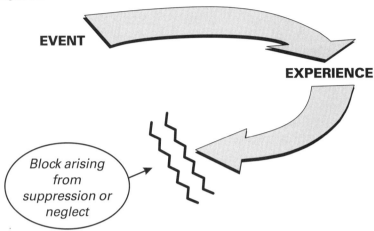

Here, the event influences the experience, but people's reaction get bottled up and don't have an opportunity to directly affect events.

Spillover

Several things happen when something blocks the flow between event and experience. First, *the blockage often makes people feel powerless*. Think of the employees whose boss told them to smile even though they knew lay-offs were coming, or the university professors who wondered which jobs and departments would be cut. These people felt—justifiably—that they were out of the loop. They had little power and couldn't influence events. They couldn't even make their concerns heard. Their spirit couldn't affect the form. The usual result is that the spirit disengages.

Just because people can't or won't express their concerns doesn't mean the concerns go away. If the boss tells his employees to smile, it doesn't mean they'll be happy. Even though no faculty member lost a job in the university's first round of cuts, the professors didn't give the administration their trust.

In the same way that garbage never really goes away, so people still experienced these events. They buried their thoughts and feelings, but the anxiety, rage, and confusion remained (figure 3–6).

Figure 3–6

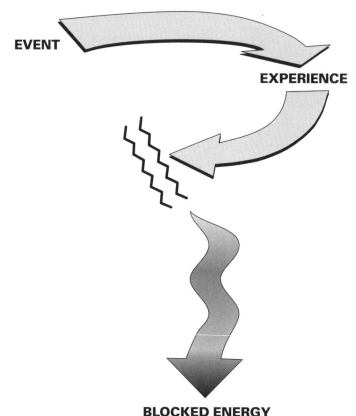

EVENT

EXPERIENCE

BLOCKED ENERGY
*(Unfinished business and
repressed experience)*

This is when blocked experience becomes so dangerous. Experience has a whole lot of energy—when you open it up, experience can generate vitality. When experience gets dammed up, it finds new directions to flow, and *the energy of blocked experience shows up in different places*.

Think back to the story of the bank, where the problem seemed to be low morale. The low morale and exhaustion were symptoms of real, deep trouble. The bank's new forms weren't working, its people had turned against one another, and no one knew where to turn for help. Because no one could talk about the difficult experience of adjusting to these new forms, all that frustration spilled out as low morale, burnout, and alienation (figure 3–7).

Figure 3–7

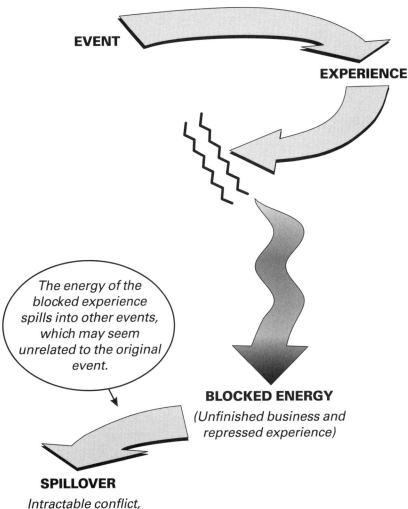

EVENT

EXPERIENCE

The energy of the blocked experience spills into other events, which may seem unrelated to the original event.

BLOCKED ENERGY

(Unfinished business and repressed experience)

SPILLOVER

Intractable conflict, disengagement, sabotage, fear, cynicism, failure of confidence, alienation, etc.

None of this should be surprising. Everyone knows the frustration of not being listened to, and of having one's questions ignored or denigrated. It's only natural that this frustration affects one's relationship with an organization.

The "spillover" problem is so common that the human resource staff of one university turned it into a running joke. Occasionally they would see a sudden rise in a department's sick days, leave requests, and resignations. They knew from these symptoms the department was having trouble—maybe administrative changes, an enrollment decline, or some kind of conflict. They would try to predict when the troubles would become public, and were usually right.

Spillover threatens organizations in a number of ways, but the most pressing danger is that spillover makes it very difficult to solve problems. *Spillover makes it seem as if an organization's problems are in one place, when in fact, those are just symptoms of the real problems, which are located somewhere else entirely.* An organization can waste a lot of time putting on Band-Aids, while its internal bleeding goes undiagnosed.

THE THIRD PRINCIPLE OF VITALITY

An organization that pays attention to people's experience can revitalize itself in even the most difficult situations.

The Research Division's Story

One of our clients was a large company's new research division. The division had been created two years earlier with great hoopla. To house it, a cutting-edge research center was built in a beautiful mountain setting. Top experts from across the country joined the division and moved their families to the area, eager to work on interesting problems for good pay. The division's vitality ran high at the start, but within two years the company shut the division down. The company had made a mistake, executives said, and wasn't going to need this research after all. The staff received lay-off notices. They'd have to clear out in six months. For everyone in the division this was, of course, a painful instance of random change.

Because the company had decided to give up on the researchers' field, it couldn't offer them other jobs, but did want to help. The best the company could offer beyond severance packages was assistance in making the transition. We were hired as part of this effort.

When we arrived, the whole division lay in torpor. People seemed stunned. The gleaming new plant had become as gloomy as some swamp in a story by Edgar Allen Poe. Our task was to help them cope with their loss as a group, and find their way forward. We conducted a three-day retreat for all ninety-one people in the division.

A few dangers crop up when a group tries to talk about experience.

First, we established an "interim form" that ensured everyone's safety and privacy (this is the first step in the Clarification process). Then we introduced the concepts of "event" and "experience". We asked people to talk about their experiences—what the plant closing meant to them personally, what it made them think and feel. Our goal was to help them "finish the business" of closing the plant, so they could move ahead intellectually and emotionally.

It wasn't always easy. There are many dangers of talking about experience, especially in a very large group like this one. Some people try to dominate the conversation, and others remain transactional by talking about events but not experience. Still others will want to intellectualize what's happened ("oh well, it's a tough world out there"). Perhaps the biggest danger is that people tend to want to move quickly toward solutions before everyone has the chance to speak. Even when everyone does speak,

Talking about experience offers direct, tangible benefits.

they might not listen as they rush to get their own thoughts out. In this group, most of the participants were male engineers, not used to discussing their feelings. There was a natural fear of becoming vulnerable.

Sometimes, people in groups also object that all this "touchy-feely" stuff kept them from their real business. We reply that dealing with experience is not an end in itself. It has direct, practical benefits, one of which is that it's a reality check. Through these discussions, an organization has a terrific opportunity to gather data about itself. Some of the things it can learn:

- *How well are its forms working?* When advertisers run focus groups to evaluate their ads, they try to discover whether the spot they have produced elicits the response they were hoping for. Does it convey the proper image of the product? Is it unintentionally offensive? These ads are forms; the focus groups test the effect on spirit. For organizations like the bank and university, workshops and speaking circles serve as internal focus groups.

- *How high or low is morale?* The safer people feel in these forums, the more honest they become. It becomes much easier to identify and measure people's satisfaction and engagement.

- *Are new ideas out there?* Front-line members of an organization often understand its problems better than anyone else, and they often know how to fix them. Unless management is genuinely interested in their ideas, people are likely to keep to themselves.

To reap the benefits of dealing with experience, a facilitator must keep the dialogue flowing and identify *themes* that arise. Doing so begins to point the group toward an understanding of what's going on beneath the surface.

At the research facility, some clear themes arose. One was that many employees were troubled to be disrupting their families' lives. They all moved here recently, and everyone had just started to settle in. Men were ashamed that they would have to uproot their wives and kids again.

A second theme was disillusionment. From the beginning, the employees had been told that this division would be the company's vanguard. Not only would it create cutting-edge technology, the division would also be the first to fully install new management methods. The hierarchy was flattened, and employees would participate in decisions. This division would become a model for the rest of the company. Now it seemed like the parent was not only selling out a division, but a promising new way of doing business. The employees appreciated their generous severance packages, except they had hoped to be corporate and technological pioneers. Those ideals had been washed away.

By the end of the first day, everyone had a chance to speak, and a consensus emerged that the group should perform a ritual to commemorate the passing of the old form. The next morning, Garvey, the division chief, brought in a large wastebasket and handed out slips of paper. Each person wrote down what they needed to let go of in order to get on with their lives. They read them aloud by turns—most said things like *anxiety, resentment, embarrassment,* or *guilt*—then dropped the paper into the trash.

They hoped this would be cathartic and cleansing, but when they finished, they felt unsatisfied. The ritual hadn't calmed the tempest they felt.

"How about a funeral?" someone suggested. People liked the idea, but no one could figure out what to bury. Finally, somebody said, "The master plan."

For two years, the employees had been working on their own master plan. This contained the division's mission statement, personnel policies, management structure, and goals. The plan was the division's ultimate form; it summarized everything they were and did, and had been on the verge of approval when the closing was announced. There was only one master copy, compiled in a three-ring binder. The vote to bury it was unanimous.

The Master Plan's Funeral

They prepared the funeral, and placed the binder in a coffin-sized cardboard box. Someone asked the custodians to dig a grave in the field behind the plant. Pallbearers hefted the coffin onto their shoulders and ninety people marched the master plan through each of the plant's buildings. On the way, Garvey quietly told us that he still had a sentimental attachment to the master plan. Would it be okay if after the funeral he returned to the field to dig it up? Sure, we said, only the symbolism matters.

Out to the field they marched, but the custodians hadn't dug a grave. Everyone stood around a little befuddled until Garvey asked, "Do you believe in cremation?"

Why not? came the reply, and somebody returned to the plant to fetch kerosene. While they waited, Chuck asked Garvey, "You sure you really want to destroy the plan?" Garvey gave a determined smile. "Let's burn it."

The "coffin" was doused with kerosene and lit. Though it burned quickly, the master plan inside remained intact. One of the pallbearers opened the binder; the plan was so thick the pages didn't catch. They had to burn it page by page, flipping through the whole thing with a stick, watching each section burn. They stood arm in arm, in a circle. Some told jokes, a few cried. There were long stretches of silence. By the end, all that remained was the metal three-ring binding, blackened and smelling of smoke.

Garvey told everyone to take the rest of the day off.

The Division Shuts Down and Moves Ahead

The next day, people were rested and ready to move ahead. Everyone agreed the issue was no longer what had happened, but what they were going to do next.

After some discussion, the division staff identified a central question: *how can we support each other during the process of shutting the division down?* Unlike most of the organizations we discuss in this book, this group had too much free time. The division would officially close in six months, and aside from mopping up a few projects, there wasn't much work to do. The first order of business was to keep intellectually stimulated and maintain a sense of community support. People volunteered to teach classes on subjects like computing, bridge, and golf. They formed discussion groups on religion, literature, and politics. They invited family members to join.

The next step was to *set up systems to help one another move out of the division.* They decided to turn the plant into a "career transition center." They hired consultants to teach resumé writing and interview techniques. They posted job openings. Everyone knew that they might be competing for the same positions, but they made a pact that they'd do their best to be supportive anyway. They agreed to notify the entire group when they went out on interviews. When anyone got a new job, the division threw a farewell party. Spouses were included in the process and received access to the same resources. (Such support is not limited to those with a luxury of time. The bank, the university, and the agriculture firm all spent a great deal of time on their revitalization.) By the end of the workshop's third day, they'd written these agreements into a two-page document they labeled "The New Master Plan."

A few months later, Garvey called us. He had promised everyone that he would be the last to leave. He wasn't sure whether he'd retire or find another job, and wanted to make sure everyone had made their way before he decided. He told us that after we'd left, the group posted a sign on the highway by the plant. On one side, they'd written "Career Transition Center." On the other, printed backward to be read in the employees' rear-view mirrors, it said, "Shit happens."

"Forty-one people have left for other jobs," Garvey said. "There are fifty left. But our morale has never been higher."

Knitting Form and Spirit Together

The irony of this story is that even as the division prepared for its own demise, it was infused with new life. The form changed completely—from research division to "career transition center"—and its spirit blossomed as the community came together.

What made this revitalization so thorough is that people engaged with the "inside"—the experience—of what was happening. Without this engagement, the group might have developed job-search services. Perhaps they might have supported one another's efforts, but as many of them told us afterward, they certainly would not have put the past behind them so well. Garvey's willingness at the funeral to burn the master plan epitomized the group's success. He had gone from wanting to hang on to the past, even if it was only for sentimental reasons, to breaking with it. Everyone had given up "Form One," and they were ready to go engage with their own "Form Two." The chaos of job searches and moves was much diminished. As a group they had a temporary "Form Two" on which to rely: the new, two-page master plan. That plan wasn't what they hoped for when they had come to the division, but it was a very effective tool, and a morale-booster as well. A form full of spirit.

In many of our stories, change separated form and spirit. Organizations like the bank, university, and research division recovered vitality by listening and responding to the experiences of their members.

Their experience is cause for hope. Vitality is achievable even against the longest odds. This is why we add a corollary to the three principles: *Vitality depends less on* what *happens to us than on* how *we deal with it.* As individuals and as organizational members, we have choices. We can control how we respond to events and what meaning we glean from them. Being attentive to experience is at the core of vitality, and is the foundation of the Clarification techniques in Part Two.

ENDNOTES

1. Wetlaufer, Suzy. "After the Layoffs, What Next?" *Harvard Business Review*, September–October 1998, pg. 26 (italics added).

✳

<u>Part Two:</u>

CLARIFICATION

INTRODUCTION

e now address practical questions: How does an organization change for the better? How do you figure out where your organization goes next? How do you build trust? How do you become a true leader, rather than just someone with a position of authority? How do you motivate employees? How do you avoid the damage that change, distrust, and poor leadership can do to vitality?

Throughout Part Two, we explain our central method in detail. This method—*Clarification*—is a flexible, step-by-step process that will help you clarify several important matters, including:

- The organization's current situation

- How people think and feel about that situation

- The influence of the past on the present

- The degree of trust or distrust in the organization

- Where the organization should go next

- and many others

While Clarification offers an excellent way to gather information, it is more than fact-finding. Clarification brings an organization's community together and gives people a way to contribute. It *engages* people. When people go through Clarification, they *take part personally* in the organization's vitality. They change personally, their personal trust and trustworthiness deepen, and they become better leaders. Clarification *brings form and spirit together*. The process of Clarification is the process of building vitality.

Chapter four, "Inside Change," introduces the principles and tools of Clarification and provides a case study of how Clarification can be used to manage change. Chapter five, "Finding a New Form," is a case study in change and how Clarification can bring about vitality.

In chapter six, "Trust," we describe how trust has an impact on

Clarification, and how Clarification in turn can build trust. Chapter seven, "Breakthrough Leadership," reveals the connection between Clarification and leadership. In particular, we offer advice to leaders at all levels—whether CEOs or janitors—who want to ignite their own spirit and improve their organization's vitality.

CLARITY

Clarification leads to *clarity*—a clear understanding of the current situation and a clear vision for the future. It clarifies what is going on with form and spirit, and reveals ways to bring form and spirit together.

The meeting of the bank presidents is an example of Clarification in action. The presidents struggled while they talked transactionally about the bank's changes. Martin, by speaking honestly about his experience, brought them real clarity. When he vented his frustrations about the new accounting systems and loan procedures, he identified critical flaws in the bank's new forms. When he said he felt "covered in blood," he put his finger on the pulse of the administrators' spirits.

His words electrified the room. More important, this new clarity about the current situation made the bank's next steps obvious. Grand, the CEO, committed himself to helping people understand and thrive during the bank's changes. He created "interim forms" such as the auditors' retreat that fostered his employees' spirits and led to stronger forms.

Clarity can come to a group—as it did with the bankers—or to an individual. The latter happened to Gordon Burns, the head of the agricultural firm. Burns had been striving to invigorate his company, but he had to swim against a current of apathy. His staff was content to be mediocre, and they greeted Burns with resentment. During one of our workshops, they complained at length to his face about his ideas and management style.

We previously talked about how Burns came into the next day's workshop ready to speak openly about his own experience. Getting ready was difficult; the day of complaints had taken its toll, and when we went out to dinner with Burns after he'd been criticized all day, he was hurt and fuming. How long would he have to put up with this? he demanded. He'd been hearing these complaints for a long time and was tired of them. He understood he had become brusque with his staff but felt they put him in that position. He'd never acted brusquely before. For years he'd been a positive, dynamic leader—why wouldn't people give him a chance? He was tired of it, he said, and starting right now, he wasn't going to take it anymore.

"I'm firing you," he told us.

We ignored him. "It's great that you're getting angry," we said. "It's about time. You have a right to your reactions, just as your staff has the right to theirs."

"I'm tired of being the bad guy," he said. "And I'm tired of listening to people tell me I'm an SOB. I don't want to work with you anymore."

"Great. It's important that you stop putting up with it, but you don't need to tell us. You need to tell your people. They need to hear your experience, just as you've heard theirs."

Later he would joke about how we ignored being "fired." That night, he reached *clarity*. He understood that in his anger and dismay over not being able to energize the company, he had shut himself off. Just like the school principal who retracted his spirit, Burns hid his humanity and idealism. Because the staff had fought his reforms, he had become a fighter, but at heart he was a collaborator.

He now knew he had to respond to the staff's attacks. More important, he *could* respond to their complaints. He could accept the legitimate criticism—maybe it was true that he'd moved too fast; maybe he had been brusque—but he was a human being, not just a boss. He had a right to feel hurt by personal attacks and as much right to say so as his staff did.

Invigorated by his understanding (his clarity), he spoke his mind the next day. When he did, his relations with the staff turned the corner and became cordial and productive. After a few months of dialogue, the group itself reached clarity. They knew which reforms to adopt and how to implement them. The process began with Burns's clarity about what he, personally, needed to do.

FOUR PREREQUISITES FOR SUCCESS

Clarity requires four things: facts, dialogue, personal reflection, and the help of a guide. Together, these four "clarifiers" can illuminate even the most chaotic of situations. We'll also see how time, space apart, safety, and other resources make Clarification possible.

Before we get to that, we need to list several requirements for vitality. The Clarification process won't work transactionally. To spark spirit, leaders cannot implement a strictly "formal" process. They have to dig into what lies beneath the surface. For that reason, vitality depends as much on the following conditions as it does on the methods we outline in the following chapters.

1. People at the top must provide unequivocal support.

In chapter three, "Three Principles of Vitality," we described a software-company CEO who said he wanted to distribute decision-making power, but in practice made all decisions himself. Everyone around him agreed he had good intentions. He really believed he wanted to push power out to his management team, yet he denied, perhaps even to himself, he was holding too tight to the reins of control. This undermined every new initiative he introduced.

> *FOUR PREREQUISITES FOR VITALITY*
>
> *1. Unequivocal support from the top.*
>
> *2. Sufficient motivation to change.*
>
> *3. Critical mass of "change agents."*
>
> *4. Follow-through.*

Soon no one trusted him, and the spirit of innovation that had begun to blossom quickly withered.

Vitality affects everyone in an organization, and keeping it alive is everyone's responsibility. Those in power have a special obligation to provide resources—time, money, space—to make the process work.

Unequivocal support doesn't only mean money and time, as important as those are. It also means that people at the top must be as engaged as everyone else. When Riley, a top manager at a restaurant chain, discovered through company surveys that his division had particularly low morale, he was compelled to take part in a workshop with his staff. On the first day, the staff complained that Riley micro-managed and never listened to them. On the second day, Riley made an announcement. He had a "solution," he said. He'd decided to hire a new manager who would act as a liaison between himself and the staff. "I know you're probably worried about adding another layer of management," he said. "I know I am, but this is the best solution."

The staff objected. No, they said, they weren't worried about a new layer of management. They were still worried about feeling ignored. Riley looked at his watch. "We've got a big agenda," he said, "and we need to move along. The decision is made." He ignored their concerns once again.

When those in power are willing to let events change them—Riley was not—they become true leaders. Tom Grand and Gordon Burns had to listen to some tough criticism, but they did listen. They changed when they had to, and when they didn't change, they explained why. That led to success. Managers who understand they are in it together with their people are not complacent about their own involvement. They don't demand that everyone *else* change while they proceed normally. They are open to the process, and they're willing to follow it. Success matters more to them than their egos.

Revitalization can be an enormous undertaking. It costs money, time, and effort, sometimes a lot of it. Managers have to be careful not to open a door to new visions, then slam it shut because crossing the threshold is difficult. The resulting disappointment quickly turns to cynicism and animosity. If there's any question about whether top decision-makers will devote their full resources to the process, it may be better not to try at all.

2. The organization needs sufficient motivation to change.

We've already talked about how difficult it can be to lose a familiar form, even if the form has outlived its usefulness. Revitalizing an organization means shaking up a lot of important forms, shaking people's spirits, and enduring a period of chaos until new forms are up and running. The road is difficult enough that most organizations need great motivation to see the trip through. They won't make it without real commitment, so they shouldn't try it because it's a neat idea or because they "ought to."

Our most successful clients are motivated by one of two factors. One, they may have very serious organizational problems (such as the bank and the university), or two, they are guided by a vision so compelling it overcomes objections (such as Gordon Burns' restructuring).

3. A critical mass of change agents needs to move the process forward.

When leadership comes spontaneously from the rank and file as well as from people in positions of authority, other members of the organization begin to attach themselves to the leaders' agenda. At a certain point, the leaders generate sufficient consensus and enthusiasm so that the whole organization begins to move with them.

This happened at a high school where faculty members asked the principal to join them in creating a "Next Step Task Force" to improve the school. The leaders agreed that "something should be done," and started exploring options. They were greeted with apathy or scorn at first, then soon were coming up with intriguing ideas and having so much fun that others joined in just to be part of the positive energy. Pretty soon, a large majority of people agreed that change should, and, more important, could happen.

It was an astounding phenomenon. We could feel the school's energy shift from cynicism to hope. It began with a few members of the rank and file who wanted to do *something*—they didn't know what—to help. The lesson is that when you reach critical mass, you don't need 100 percent buy-in. Those who obstinately resist the process get isolated; even factions that have blocked new initiatives for years lose their power to obstruct change.

4. The organization must provide follow-through.

When the new director of a non-profit announced he planned a complete restructuring and that he wanted input, the staff responded enthusiastically. They researched their past and present conditions, talked about their experiences, and made scores of suggestions. Two years later, they were still waiting for a response. The director had apparently dropped his plans, but never told the staff why or even that he'd done so. He reaped a field of cynicism.

The moral of the story is, "don't start what you won't finish." When people put their spirits on the line, the forms they're engaging with had better repay their investment.

All too often, organizations unleash astounding spirit only to let it dribble away. Leaders who want to harness vitality need to develop concrete follow-through strategies. Without a plan to keep it engaged, spirit dissipates quickly.

IV ✳ INSIDE CHANGE

ugene Glenn was appointed to reform the sluggish bureaucracy of a government agency. Employees had to fill out forms and await their bosses' approval for everyday tasks. Requisitioning a sheaf of photocopies required two weeks' lead time. Hiring could take three months, which meant that after a departing employee gave two weeks notice, the open position might remain unfilled for a quarter of a year. Not surprisingly, surveys revealed abysmal levels of customer and employee satisfaction.

Glenn was convinced he could, as the saying went, reinvent this corner of government. He'd done the same in the private sector and with other government entities. Anyway, he didn't have much choice. The agency was the target of so many complaints that elected officials held hearings to investigate its performance. The legislature had been so dismayed by its findings that it considered privatizing the agency. Instead, they gave the agency one last chance: the agency had five years to transform itself into an organization that delivered measurable, high levels of customer service to the public.

The agency had been structured as a top-down hierarchy, with political bosses on top, rank-and-file bureaucrats beneath, and the public often treated as paperwork to be shuffled through the system. A hundred years earlier, when the agency had been founded amid widespread government corruption and nepotism, such a hierarchy prevented abuse of the system. But the bureaucratic form had worn itself out; rather than making the agency work better, the bureaucracy clogged it. Now the institution would have to re-orient itself completely. The public would become "customers," and customers, not administrators, would come first. Employees needed new skills, freedom, and power, plus the resources to meet customers' needs. Many employees would be shuffled into new work units. The agency's structure would be dismantled and rebuilt, its procedures streamlined. Nearly every form would change.

Glenn knew this wasn't even half the battle. The spirit had to change, too. The transactional, bureaucratic spirit would have to give way to one that was energetic and vital. This would be a complete transformation.

The organization as it had existed would disappear, and another would replace it.

Though the legislature's mandate gave Glenn authority to make sweeping changes, he knew the transition would be exceptionally difficult. The agency had become so ossified that simply changing computers was an ordeal. Change the whole culture? For Glenn—and for all leaders who want to carry out a revitalizing change—the real trick was to build new forms in a way that enhanced spirit.

There is rarely a direct line between one form and the next. A period of chaos intervenes as people adjust to new forms. Familiar routines are lost. People get disoriented as they try to figure out their new roles, and are often skeptical of investing spirit into forms they don't know. It was going to be, said Glenn's top lieutenant Nancy Baird, *messy*.

Glenn and Baird hired dozens of consultants to overhaul the organizational chart, computer systems, and job descriptions. We were brought in as part of this reforming herd. As subcontractors and colleagues of the Public Strategies Group (PSG), a real-life organization that consults with governments, our job would be to work with front-line employees—the people who encountered the public on a daily basis—and the managers and staff who supported them. It was this group, one thousand strong, whose jobs would change the most. PSG and the agency asked us to train these folks. We taught them how to assess and meet customer expectations, and helped them make the psychological move from the old form to the new.

The agency's story is an excellent case study in our core technique of Clarification. The Clarification process eventually moved a critical mass of employees toward new forms. Clarification helped them understand the changes around them, and allowed them to engage—safely—with Glenn's vision of a new agency. This chapter describes how Clarification works. Chapter five, "Finding a New Form," explains how we applied it at the agency.

PRINCIPLES AND TOOLS OF CLARIFICATION

One at a Time

The premise of our work with the agency was that *true organizational change occurs only when individuals change*.

Earlier we described the "transactional culture"—a climate in which attention is placed only on forms, not on spirit. It is equally possible to engage in "transactional change," in which the forms change but the spirit doesn't change with them. A handful of bosses can decree—as Glenn and Baird did—that all of an organization's forms will be overhauled. To make the change *transformational* rather than transactional, the rest of the organization (shareholders, employees, suppliers, and customers) must buy in. Many people need to invest in the new forms. Each individual is faced with the choice of whether and how deeply to invest spirit. The bosses can lead them to new forms, but they can't make them engage.

The question of buy-in was especially important at the agency, because the most significant change would be in the hearts and minds of front-line employees. They would have to transform the way they interacted with the public, and take more initiative to help customers. The administrators could demand customer service all they wanted, but ultimately, it was up to the individual rank and file members to make it happen.

> *True organizational change occurs one person at a time. If individuals do not invest in new forms, then forms are the only things that will change. Spirit won't come along for the ride.*

People can invest in form to varying degrees, ranging from low-grade "involvement" to deeper "commitment" and "identification." Here at the agency, just being "involved"—showing up and going through the motions—would be insufficient to satisfy alienated customers. Glenn needed people to be committed to, even identify with, their customers' satisfaction.

This is true for most organizations. The auditors at the bank had to become *committed* to helping (rather than overseeing) their colleagues in the branch offices. Eventually they "identified" themselves not simply as investigators, but as guides and tutors. For most organizations, getting individuals deeply invested in a new form is not optional. It must be done.

For the employees, however, the choice of whether to commit to the change *was* optional. Each person could embrace or reject new forms. The agency's front-line people could continue to treat customers as an afterthought. If enough people fail to embrace the change, the change won't take hold. This creates an obvious dilemma: how does an organization get people to commit to or identify with new forms, when it can't force them?

> ### THE CHALLENGE FOR ORGANIZATIONS
>
> *How can you get people to invest deeply in new forms when you can't force them?*

An organization can reward people who embrace the change by offering raises or promotions, for instance. It can punish those who reject the change. Both strategies are effective to a point. The best incentive for change is when people find *personal meaning* in new forms. Change becomes its own reward. The bank auditors changed because becoming mentors was more meaningful and enriching than being The Enemy. By finding a form that meant something to them, they became much more engaged and effective than if they had been motivated only by money or fear.

Clarification: A Method for Transformation

To find meaning—a payoff for spirit—in the agency's new forms, the employees needed two things: information and a personal sense of their places in the change.

First, let's look at information. To engage with the agency's new forms, the employees would have to understand, inside and out, how those new forms worked. They needed to know *what* was going to change, also, *who* was making the decisions and would be affected by them. *How* would the change be implemented, and *when*? *Why* had the change been mandated? Why the move toward one customer-service model as opposed to another? The employees required a vision, a glimpse of the new forms and the road ahead.

At the agency, people were clamoring for this information. In our early workshops, we encountered a fusillade of questions. "How do we know our customers aren't satisfied?" "How do we know this isn't just another training fad?" "How will the agency be restructured?"

Factual information was necessary, but it wasn't sufficient to create true transformation. People needed a sense of their personal place in the change.

> *To embrace change, people need a personal stake in the new forms. The forms must mean something to them personally.*

Facts can help people *accept and understand* the change, but they need much more to *embrace* it. People had to feel that the benefits would outweigh the risks. They needed to have a stake in the new forms—a sense that the forms rewarded their investment of spirit and gave their work meaning.

The employees wondered how the changes would affect them personally. Would there be lay-offs? Would their job descriptions change? Would they answer to new bosses or be evaluated by new standards? Did this big change imply that in the past they hadn't been good enough? Many employees were simultaneously cynical and anxious. They sneered at the idea that the agency could actually change after decades of inertia, but they were also alarmed by the possibility that it might change, mainly because it meant that *they themselves* would have to change. While a lot of questions were about facts, even more were about people's "experience" of events, about the "inside" of the change.

If people were to fully engage in the new forms, we would have to deal with both sides of the change—the outside and the inside, the events and the experience. Clarification would let us explore both of these sides (figure 4–1).

Figure 4–1

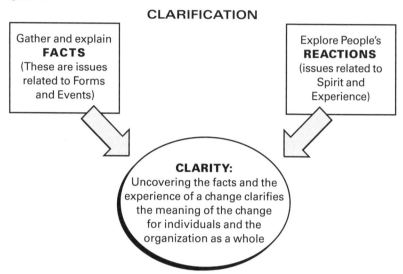

CLARIFICATION

Gather and explain
FACTS
(These are issues
related to Forms
and Events)

Explore People's
REACTIONS
(issues related to
Spirit and
Experience)

CLARITY:
Uncovering the facts and the
experience of a change clarifies
the meaning of the change
for individuals and the
organization as a whole

Clarification is essentially the process of determining the facts of a situation and discovering people's reactions to those facts. In the process, people become engaged in the change; they put the past to rest; they discover the personal meaning of the change; and they are forced to decide whether to invest spirit in new forms.

BENEFITS OF CLARIFICATION

We call our method Clarification because it *clarifies the situation* by laying out the facts and exposing hidden dynamics (such as the school principal's hostility toward the teachers, or Martin's feeling he was "covered in blood"). It helps people understand what is going on. They understand what is going on with the organization as a whole, what is going on inside other people, and where they as individuals fit into the bigger picture. Clarification helps people discern *what the situation means to the organization and to themselves personally*. Clarification also offers more than clarity by getting things done. To be specific:

1. Clarification *gets people engaged*. At the university, the "speaking circles" engaged people in conversations about improving the school. Once they were engaged in the reform process, keeping them involved was much easier. At the agency, we had a similar goal: to get burned-out, cynical em-

ployees excited to learn about and discuss the changes around them.

> ### BENEFITS OF CLARIFICATION
>
> *1. It clarifies the present situation.*
>
> *2. It gets people engaged.*
>
> *3. It puts the past to rest.*
>
> *4. People reach a decisive moment when they must decide whether to invest spirit in the organization.*

2. Clarification *puts the past to rest.* Unfinished business and unresolved conflicts can drag down an organization's vitality. Clarification gives people a safe, effective way of resolving old disputes and rectifying past mistakes.

3. *Clarification brings people to a decisive moment.* When they reach clarity, people understand their situation in very personal terms. They understand where and how they will personally fit into the whole picture. They know what they will gain and what they will lose, and they are forced to decide whether they will get aboard for the changes and invest in the new forms.

In the end, some people refuse to change. At the decisive moment, they will quit or fight. That doesn't matter. Most people do find meaning in progress, and they do change. Clarification brings people to this moment of decision where they know what the change means. From there, most of them accept the change, and a significant number of spontaneous leaders and visionaries will actually engage to help make the change a reality.

All of these benefits arise from the process of clarifying facts and exploring people's reactions to those facts.

CRITICAL MASS

The spontaneous leaders and visionaries who help bring about change (or increased trust) do the most important work. Their energy and enthusiasm pull others along. As the graphs below illustrate (figures 4–2 and 4–3), doubters and resisters become increasingly isolated as the organization achieves a *critical mass* of individuals who want to engage in the new forms.

Figure 4–2

BEFORE ACHIEVING CRITICAL MASS:
Where People First Stand

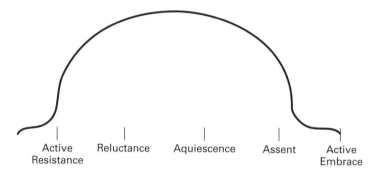

| Active Resistance | Reluctance | Aquiescence | Assent | Active Embrace |

This bell curve illustrates the average positions of people regarding a proposed change. A few people enthusiastically embrace the change from the beginning. Others fight against it from the start. Most are somewhere in the middle. They may be curious, willing to give the change a try, or indifferent.

Figure 4–3

MOVING THE MASS

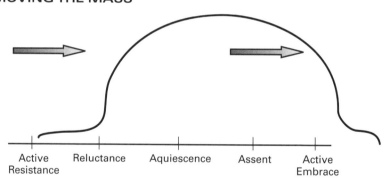

| Active Resistance | Reluctance | Aquiescence | Assent | Active Embrace |

After Clarification, the bell curve shifts toward greater acceptance of the new form. The goal of change management is not to get every member of the organization on board, it is to get the active engagement of a critical mass of spontaneous leaders. These leaders' spirited investment in the new form will "move the middle," bringing the majority of people at least toward curiosity and acceptance of the change. Resisters will remain, but in low numbers. With most people moving ahead, the resisters will find themselves at odds with the organization's entire culture.

Clarification creates this critical mass of people who will build trust and carry the organization through change.

Clarification is flexible in its applications. We came to the project with the government agency to help train employees in customer satisfaction. Clarification can be used for other applications, too. The university used Clarification to figure out its real mission. The agriculture firm used it to transform its traditional, self-enclosed departments into cross-disciplinary units. The high-tech firm used it to close out its own existence.

We are not experts in customer service, streamlining, or organizational restructuring. It is our job to help organizations figure out where they want to go and help get them there. The agency's goal was to improve customer service, but this book is not about customer service. It's about bringing *spirit* and *meaning* into reality. As a result, we spend very little time describing the customer-service techniques the agency adopted. To us, the most important thing is not the "what," but the "how."

INTERIM FORMS AS ARENAS FOR TRANSFORMATION

The first step in Clarification is to establish an arena to explore facts and reactions. This arena is a temporary *interim form* (perhaps a workshop, training session, or retreat) where individuals can be transformed.

Interim forms are temporary forms that bridge the gap between one relatively permanent form and another. Interim forms are like ferry boats. You use them to cross the rapids of chaos, and once you reach the far bank, you leave them behind.

In all the stories we've told, the key moment of transformation occurred within interim forms. At the bank, the presidents' meeting and the auditors' retreat were temporary arenas put together for the specific purpose of dealing with change.

A variety of interim forms can be effective. Some we've seen include the following:

1. Two-and-a-half-day workshops.
While two and a half days are rarely enough time to institute real change, it is sufficient to make good progress. On the first evening, we make intro-

ductions, lay out the agenda, answer questions, and describe our "contract for safety." We often encourage participants to consider a few open-ended questions about their situation. The next morning we step right into a full day of dialogue or negotiation. These conversations can end up dead-locked; even when they're harmoni-ous and productive, they frequently lead to a moment when no one knows what should come next. When we take them up again on the third day, people have had time to rest, process the previous day's flurry of ideas, and back away from unreasonable stanc-es. Third days are almost always the most productive.

Interim forms are temporary forms that help preserve order when traditional forms are in disarray. They are also great places to engage people in moving forward.

For a good example of this kind of workshop, recall our work at the high-tech plant. On the first day, we introduced our ideas of form, spirit, and change. The second day brought on a powerful dialogue about people's sense of loss, followed by the "funeral" for the Master Plan. On the third day, people returned refreshed and ready to begin again, and in just a few hours the division decided to re-invent itself as a career place-ment center.

2. An extended "period of transition."

The suburban church that lost its pastor declared a three-month period of transition. During that time, the staff interviewed every congregation member and developed a list of priorities that culminated in the hiring of a new pastor.

3. Any interim position.

"Interim president," is an interim form. The position bridges the gap be-tween one stable form and the next.

4. A team of change agents.

In the introduction and chapter seven, we describe the "Next Step Task Force" of school employees. The task force is an interim form, created to spark change, and lasted as long as it took to move through that change. A similar team of employee "coaches" worked at the agency. These were rank and file employees enthusiastic about customer satisfaction who wanted to help transform the organization. During our workshops, they helped us lead discussions and acted as role models for other employees.

The basic interim form at the agency was a series of training workshops. We would lead several series. In the original plan, each series was to last six sessions (one session a week), with fifty participants per series. We would go until every agency employee had attended at least one six-session program. (Later the plan would reduce the number of sessions from six to five, and cut the time of each session from four hours to three.)

These sessions provided facts, answered questions, let people talk about their experiences, and taught the participants how to use customer-satisfaction tools. The employees attended with their regular work unit—every member of the information technology office, for instance, came in together and sat at the same table. Each session lasted half a day, once a week. Between sessions, we assigned real-world "homework" that required the groups to practice providing customer satisfaction.

> **THE AGENCY'S INTERIM FORM**
>
> *Five training sessions*
>
> *One session per week*
>
> *Three hours per session*
>
> **Every employee in attendance**

We will talk later about why the program was put together like this. For now, we only need note that the interim forms your organization will use—whether they're a series of workshops or a single retreat or a task force—depend on the organization's needs and resources.

CHAOS REDUX

Interim forms are important practically and psychologically. In practical terms, a good interim form provides a clear, specific way to address change. When information is scarce and communication crucial, interim forms offer an efficient way to exchange data and start a dialogue.

Psychologically, interim forms may be even more important. Scholars such as William Bridges have described a period of adjustment and confusion when old forms no longer work but new ones have yet to be established. We call this middle zone "Chaos" (figure 4–4).

Figure 4–4

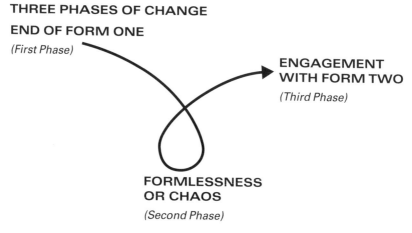

THREE PHASES OF CHANGE
END OF FORM ONE
(First Phase)

ENGAGEMENT WITH FORM TWO
(Third Phase)

FORMLESSNESS OR CHAOS
(Second Phase)

During the Chaos phase, the world seems cloudy, even senseless. People don't know what to expect. The forms they've relied on no longer foster spirit. New forms have not yet appeared or look unreachable.

To set up a good interim form sends people a message that the organization is doing *something*. The organization acknowledges the chaos, and provides whatever stability and security it can. A good interim form reassures people it's natural for them to be experiencing chaos and also provides a means for finding their way out of it.

What, then, makes a good interim form? How do you build one? The exact shape of any interim form depends on the organization, but four elements—safety, time, space apart, and sufficient resources—must always be present.

To make an interim form an arena for Clarification and not just one more meeting or workshop or task force, the organization must guarantee

> ## THE ARENA'S FOUR WALLS
>
> The "Four Walls" of a good interim form
>
> Safety
>
> Time
>
> Space
>
> Other resources

safety, space apart, time, and other resources.

Together, these elements act as boundaries of the form (figure 4–5). Outside the boundaries are the distractions of the regular world. Inside, people can concentrate on transformation. Without these "walls," Clarification and real change are next to impossible.

Figure 4–5

THE FOUR WALLS OF CLARIFICATION

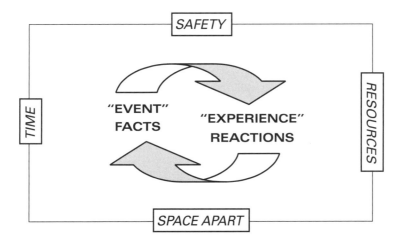

This illustration shows the basic structure of an interim form used for Clarification. The interim form—which could be any form from a training session to a retreat to a lengthy "period of transition"—establishes the "four walls" of safety, time, space apart, and resources. Within these walls, people are able to learn about, respond to, and discover the meaning of their situation.

Safety

> *A good interim form helps cope with chaos. It creates a sense of order and stability, but also gives people a place and time to deal directly with the chaos. By confronting chaos within the safety of an interim form, people can overcome it.*

Safety is the *most important ingredient* of Clarification. People *must* feel safe if they are going to speak honestly. More than likely, they will begin the Clarification process feeling anything but safe.

On one of the first days of the training session, several agency employees were mingling near the entrance of the conference center. Nearby was a group of people no one had met, probably participants of another conference. The unknown group was taking photos and some of the agency folks panicked. They stormed inside, scared and furious because, they said, they were under "surveillance" by management. At first we thought they were kidding. After all, management had required every employee to attend; they didn't need spies to know who would receive the training. The employees were dead serious. We had to repeatedly assure them that what they said would not be used against them.

To ensure safety, we built a number of precautions into the training sessions, as we do in all of our work. We call these precautions, collectively, our *contract for safety*.

> *We establish a "contract for safety" to help ensure that every participant understands the value we place on a safe, trustworthy environment.*

Our central promise is to maintain privacy. When we present our final report, we speak only in general terms about what was said. We rarely quote anyone directly, and if we do, we never reveal the quote's source. (This is why we do not name organizations in this book.) We also ask participants to abide by the same rules. They're free to express their opinions about the workshop, and they may talk about what was discussed, but we urge them to respect their colleagues' privacy, even if revealing what someone said seems innocuous. (Occasionally, someone does let something "harmless" slip, and it can take weeks to clean up the mess.) The stakes, real and perceived, are too high for even well-intentioned revelations. With few exceptions, we do not allow visitors. We identify ourselves and anyone who is working with us.

Depending on the situation, we may add further precautions. At the agency, distrust between management and the rank and file was running high enough to endanger open discussion. We instituted a "no managers" clause, and management received separate training. (Normally, we prefer to bring together a cross-section of the entire organization. At the agency, this wouldn't have worked, one example of why there's no one "right" interim form for all organizations.)

Safety is largely a subjective, not objective, condition. People who are safe may not always *feel* safe. The participants who feared the photographers were over-reacting, and telling them this would not make them feel any safer. Instead, we listened to their fears and took steps to address them. This approach built trust between us.

The contract for safety isn't so much a static agreement as it is a promise to provide a climate of safety and trust. To speak honestly is to risk being disliked, laughed at, or labeled as a trouble-maker or brown-noser. It is essential that people trust if they are to be open and grow.

Space Apart

By "space apart" we mean a place free of the demands and distractions of the daily routine. Clarification requires concentrated effort, impossible to find when the cell phone is chiming, colleagues poke their heads in for "just one quick question," and a trip to the bathroom can turn into an impromptu hallway meeting.

There's more to the space issue than preventing distractions. Going to a new place can set a tone of mission. It says, "we're embarked on something new. This isn't business as usual."

Even more important, space apart connects to the question of safety. When you want people to speak frankly, you must create a safe environment. Getting them out of their offices and cubicles, away from prying eyes and ears, can go a long way toward building their confidence.

What sort of space to use depends on the nature of the change. At the university, we set up our "speaking circles" in convenient locations because we needed as many participants as possible. We didn't want to be too formal; we wanted to welcome, not intimidate people. Most of the speaking circles were hosted in classrooms. On the other hand, the auditors' retreat needed to offer rest, hope, and privacy to burned-out people. We took them to a resort.

At the agency, we used a conference center located about a mile from the regular offices. Employees were shuttled over for free or drove on their own. This addressed the competing concerns of convenience and the need—extremely pronounced among agency employees—for a safe, discreet location.

Time

Of all four Clarification "walls," time is the most ambiguous and complicated. People need sufficient time to learn facts, ask and answer questions, and figure out where they stand. Some will reach clarity quickly, others will need more focused attention, but everyone requires some time to move through chaos to new forms.

Still, the world and competition move quickly and no organization can afford to squander its time. It has to move rapidly and decisively. It needs people to "get it" ASAP.

This dilemma challenged our efforts to plan the training sessions at the agency. We had to provide focused attention for nearly 1000 employees. They needed time to ask questions and raise objections, and to practice the new customer-service techniques we were teaching. Simultaneously, the legislators who required the transition to customer-service standards were demanding a progress report within four months. The agency was being squeezed on both sides by time pressures. It needed to give the employees plenty of time to work, but didn't have much time to spare.

The schedule we settled on met both those needs. During our pilot program, we led people through six sessions. Afterward, we cut back to five,

Time is a challenging issue. Organizations need to give people time to learn facts and react to events. On the other hand, no organization can afford to squander its time.

because the benefits of a sixth session were not worth the additional time. We also reduced the sessions from four to three hours. To compensate for the lost time, we brought in a few extra facilitators to make sure every participant received the assistance they needed. Plus, we relied on volunteer employee-coaches to offer extra guidance. Most employees received fifteen hours of Clarification and training spread out over five weeks. We hosted two groups of employees a day, three days a week, and this allowed us to speed about 1000 people through the program in two and a half months.

It is possible to devote significant time to Clarification and still get work done. Although we reduced the time commitment after the pilot program, we did it with full confidence we could still give people what they needed. We were not willing to compromise any further.

A major consideration was down-time. We could have given groups fifteen hours of training over two consecutive days, but we decided to spread the sessions out because we didn't want to overload people, and we wanted them to think about and put into practice the material we covered each week. The time between sessions allowed deeper, more specific questions to emerge as people worked with the material during the week.

Down-time is integrated into our work whenever we can. A vital part of our three-day workshops is the opportunity for people to "sleep on it." Such personal reflection is crucial for people to find meaning in what they are doing, to incorporate what they've learned, and put it into the context of their own lives. While Clarification can bring chaos and conflict to the surface, down-time gives people an opportunity to cool off and work out solutions.

After the second-day "funeral" for the Master Plan at the high-tech plant, for example, we could have gone back to work to discuss next steps, but this would have been foolish. Everyone was exhausted and emotionally spent. The most efficient way to spend that time was by *not* working, so we gave them the afternoon off. Down-time helped people cope with the stress of changing their hearts and minds. It gave them time to adjust from thinking about the past to envisioning the future.

If you still don't trust the value of down-time, remember the basic rule of exercise: *you get stronger during rest and recovery*. Weightlifters know that their exercise exhausts their muscles. When they rest, the muscles recover from the stress and become stronger. If the muscles don't have a chance to rest, muscles eventually break down and weaken. The same is true of mental and emotional stress: when we rest, we become stronger. Otherwise, we exhaust our strength.[1]

Other Resources

The success of any interim form depends on a variety of other resources. The most significant are:

1. Money.

Putting on workshops or retreats can cost a lot. There may be consultants or trainers to hire. You may need to purchase supplies and tools, and there is the notable expense of paying employees for time they spend off-line.

We incorporate down-time and recovery time into all our work. This allows people to reflect and incorporate what they've learned.

2. Logistical support.

So many people went through our training at the agency that the administration assigned two full-time employees to handle logistics. They arranged shuttles to the conference center, photocopied handouts, put together information packets, ordered beverages and snacks, and ran countless errands to meet participants' needs. Even when the Clarification is smaller in scope, there are many details that need attention.

3. Intangibles.

In the introduction to this section, we said that one condition for generating vitality was unequivocal support from the top. This support shows itself in the resources we've listed, and also in intangibles: a clearly articulated vision, openness to questions and constructive criticism, fairness, flexibility, and a willingness on the part of the top echelon to move among the people. Some of the most powerful, transformative moments at the agency occurred when Eugene Glenn, Nancy Baird, or another top administrator came to the training sessions to talk with the employees. They fielded tough questions without becoming defensive, laid out their vision and left no doubt that the organization was going to move ahead, exhorted the employees to be bold, and sought people's input. They didn't just set an agenda from their top floor offices. They got down in the trenches, which made a critical difference.

FOUR CLARIFIERS: FACTS, PERSONAL REFLECTION, DIALOGUE, AND GUIDANCE

By the time we met with the first group of employees, we had established most of the "walls" of our Clarification arena. We had a separate space, sufficient time, and enough resources to get the job done, and created conditions where people would *be* safe to speak openly, though it remained to make them *feel* safe. Creating a safe feeling would be one of the tasks of the first session—as it is in any Clarification effort.

Safety, space, time, and resources are only means to an end. The goal of Clarification is to clarify what happened in the past, what is happening at present, and what will happen. Even more, it is to understand what all this *means* to each person and team. The "four walls" provide an arena in which to explore those questions, but how is this exploring done?

We try to establish a flow between event and experience, and to do this, we depend on another foursome. Clarity can be achieved through a combination of

1. Learning the facts

2. Personal reflection

3. Dialogue

4. Guidance and help

Figure 4–6

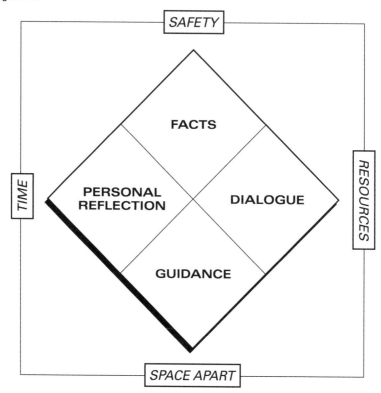

We have already noted that Clarification is a matter of exploring events and experiences within the "four walls." This diagram gets more specific about how to explore. First, the facts of the situation are established so that everyone understands them. Second, people reflect on their personal experiences. Third, they discuss those experiences and the facts in open, honest dialogue. Finally, a guide raises and answers questions, facilitates dialogue, notices "themes" in the conversation, and provides extra help when the process bogs down.

Later we'll look at specific examples of how each of these elements leads to clarity, so for now we will only give each a brief introduction.

Facts: Facts include everything from the organization's financial situation and its competitors' activities to particular "events." Facts can be slippery, especially during times of change and confusion. Two people may see the same situation so differently that it's hard to determine what the facts really are. In chapter seven, "Breakthrough Leadership," we'll examine four categories of fact in detail: economic and legal realities, organizational history, organizational processes, and people and their experiences.

Personal Reflection: Participants in the workshops consider their own experience of the events at hand. People need an opportunity to ponder what the situation means to them personally. What is their place in the organization, and will it change? Do they *want* to change? What do they hope for or fear?

Dialogue: Understanding the facts and reflecting on their meaning provides a platform for dialogue. This dialogue is important for a couple of reasons. It is impossible to understand what's going on in an organization without understanding what others are experiencing. When Martin said he was "covered in blood," he helped Grand understand what was going on in the bank. Dialogue also helps people understand not only where others are at, but how they themselves think and feel. Martin's statement helped the other branch presidents identify their own frustrations, and gave them permission to think their own thoughts.

Guidance: Getting people to reflect and talk *productively* is the role of a guide or facilitator. Keeping the dialogue on-subject can get tricky, and it's important that someone with experience be present. Additionally, certain groups or individuals may have particular trouble understanding or coping with a change; they'll need extra help.

Who should serve as guide? The most effective guidance comes from a combined team of internal and external facilitators. At the agency, several volunteer employee-coaches helped us run the workshops, and they were invaluable assets. They knew the agency's history and office politics, they did excellent work, and their enthusiasm gave the process credibility. These volunteers couldn't have done it on their own, partly because they didn't have the time or training—they were still doing their regular jobs on top of coaching—and because they themselves were enmeshed in the chaos of the overhaul. Outside facilitators aren't directly affected by the changes afoot and can often see the situation more clearly, plus they have training and experience. A combined team limits the shortcomings and enhances the strengths of both insiders and outsiders.

SUMMARY

In this chapter, we've seen that true change occurs one person at a time. An organization can change its forms at will but can't change people's spirits. Only the people themselves can do that.

Clarification is a process that makes this deeper transformation possible. The ultimate purpose of Clarification is to build a critical mass of people who engage with the organization's new forms. The road to critical mass goes like this:

1. An organization *establishes interim forms* that give people safety, time, space apart, and other resources, which create order amid the chaos of change.

2. These interim forms give people the facts about the present situation. They also let people reflect on and talk about that situation. Unfinished business gets aired. Buried conflicts come to the surface and are resolved. In this way, the past as well as the present become clear, and the future becomes clearer too, as people discuss visions for the future and get their questions answered. In this way, *Clarification clarifies*.

3. People become *engaged in the process* of Clarification. They get involved in learning what's going on and talking about it. Because they are engaged and feel their voices are being heard, they are more likely to invest in the organization's new forms later.

4. When people become clear about where the organization has been, where it is, and where it's going, they reach a *decisive moment*. They understand what all this means to them personally, and they must choose whether to embrace the organization's new forms or reject them.

5. If the new forms reward spirit, more people will engage. Finally, *a critical mass of people* will invest in the change, and the resisters are isolated and lose power. The people will have changed their spirits and invested in the organization's new forms.

We have also seen that Clarification takes place within the "four walls" of safety, time, space, and other resources. Within those "walls," which make up an interim form, people are free to explore the events and experience of their situation. Specifically, they do that exploration with the help of four clarifiers: facts, personal reflection, dialogue, and guidance.

In the next chapter, we'll show just how these four clarifiers operate within the four walls, and we'll give specific examples and suggestions for making Clarification work.

ENDNOTES

1. James E. Loehr, *Toughness Training for Life* (New York: Plume/ Penguin, 1994) offers an excellent exploration of the concept of getting tougher through a combination of stress and recovery.

V ✳ FINDING A NEW FORM

sing the story of the government agency, this chapter describes how to set up the "four walls" of an interim form (safety, time, space, and other resources) and how to explore events and experience using the "four clarifiers" (facts, reflection, dialogue, and guidance).

We held several workshops for the agency, each series consisting of one three-hour workshop a week for five weeks. After a session, we would debrief with the employee-coaches and our colleagues, who helped us evaluate what was going on and how we could do better. The events that were typical of each workshop are described, and we take time for debriefing afterward to discuss some of the reasons why we did things and their implications. Throughout, we show how Clarification gets people engaged, brings them clarity about what change means to them, and develops a critical mass of people to establish new forms.

THE FIRST SESSION: "I HATE FIRST DAYS"

On the first day of our training sessions at the agency, we introduced ourselves and the employee-coaches assisting us, laid out the agenda for that day and future sessions, and explained the contract for safety. All of this information established our "four walls." It told people how their time would be used, what we would do with this meeting space, what other resources (like snacks and booklets) would be provided, and most important, told them this was a safe place. Then we got right into the "four clarifiers" (facts, reflection, dialogue, and guidance).

Facts

First, we explained some facts. The single most important fact was why we were there. We explained the administration's vision of a customer satisfaction-based organization, and gently but firmly made it clear that this change had to go forward. We explained the legislature's mandate and pointed to other evidence that the administration was serious (not least that Glenn and Baird received bonuses if they produced results). Besides giving information, these facts helped persuade people the focus on customer satisfaction was not a fad to soon pass away. Change was really happening and people had to get aboard or be left behind. They may or may not like the change, but couldn't deny it was happening.

The next step was to get people *engaged* in talking about facts and in reflection and dialogue. Each work unit had to come up with two lists: "What do you know about the customer-satisfaction initiative?" and "What questions do you have?" People could ask any question they wanted to about the changes. We would present the questions to Glenn, Baird, and other administrators, who would answer them later.

At one level, this assignment was designed to deal with facts. By asking people to list what they knew and what they didn't know, we would be able to identify knowledge gaps where the facts weren't clear. People did have questions about basic facts. "Will my office be moved?" was one. "How will our performance be evaluated in the new system?" was another.

On another level, the assignment was to get people engaged. Everyone had questions, and this was a way to get people thinking and talking without intimidating them. It gave them a stake in the process.

Explaining facts and letting people ask questions is important in its own right, but also gets people engaged in the interim form of the workshop.

People did engage, sometimes at a deep level. Many of the questions weren't simply about facts. They were statements about where people were at, and began to reveal experience.

Some questions were skeptical ("Why should we believe this training is any different than all the others we've been through?") and others hopeful ("How quickly will we see results?").

Many questions were downright hostile. Some participants used the questions as weapons, unleashing what seemed like years of pent-up resentment, anger, and cynicism. "If I save the agency money," someone asked, "do I get part of Eugene Glenn's bonus?" Somebody else wondered, "Why are we spending money on this training when I don't have a good computer?" Another moaned, "What did I do to deserve this?"

These questions helped us and the administrators understand what was going on with the employees. They helped the employees learn the facts. By letting people voice their confusion, hope, skepticism, and even hostility, these questions got people involved. They may have felt lost or angry, but at least they were thinking and talking about it.

Reflection

We followed the question period by delving even more directly into experience. First, we provided an opportunity for personal reflection. We gave each participant a small stack of Post-It notes. "Write your reactions," we asked. "Anything about the agency or customer satisfaction or about being at this workshop."

The Post-Its allowed people to remain anonymous—a tactic we hoped would encourage honesty. People filled them out, then left them to be collected by the coaches, who read them aloud. Again, the reactions ranged from hope to skepticism to fury. Many people didn't need anonymity to express themselves. "I don't want to be here," one woman complained aloud. "All I want is to do my job and get paid so I can take care of my family." Another, a travel auditor, complained, "I'd rather give birth to ten babies than be in this training." These reactions are typical. Opening the door to chaos is like setting a rodeo bull loose in the room. When people encounter chaos, their reaction is generally anxiety, resentment, and resistance. The impulse when faced with change is to say, in one way or another, "No!"

As we moved from personal reflection to dialogue—the full force of resistance, frustration, and cynicism poured out. People were angry they had to be at the workshop, and about how the agency was run. Some brought up twelve-year-old grudges.

> *Opening the door to chaos is like setting a rodeo bull loose in the room.*

The volunteer coaches were stunned. They had never experienced anything like it. Even those of us who'd seen it all before felt besieged. Larry Grant of Public Strategies Group said afterward, "I hate first days." Larry's comment bespeaks long, tiring experience. He also recognizes that first days are just that—the first of many—and things will improve. His experience, like ours, is "People aren't going to hear what you have to say until they know you've heard them." We promised to pass people's questions and reactions on to the administration. We promised to get them answers, and thanked everyone for speaking their minds.

People will listen to you and your plans only when they believe that you have heard them and their concerns.

The last major task of the day was to describe the three stages of change. We showed everyone the "Form One–Chaos–Form Two" diagram introduced in chapter two, "Form and Spirit's Difficult Road." Form One—in this case, the old bureaucracy—had its place, but outlived its usefulness. Before Form Two was up and running, there would be chaos.

"You're already familiar with that chaos," we said. "When you complain that the agency is spending money on training when you don't have an adequate computer, you're talking about chaos. This is a messy time. Things don't always fit or make sense. Many of you are angry, confused, or cynical. That's natural. We're not asking you to pretend to be anything different. Wherever you're at, it's okay to be there. This is a very difficult process, and a lot is being asked of you. However you feel, we encourage you to keep exploring it. Talk about it, think about it, and try to figure out what all this means to you personally."

We closed the session by assigning homework to encourage reflection. Everyone was to write down three columns of material (figure 5–1): first, elements of "form one," the current bureaucracy they regularly encountered; second, the elements of chaos that infected the organization; and third, their visions of what a customer-satisfaction orientation would look like. Finally, they were to circle any elements of Form One that would work well in Form Two.

Figure 5–1

FORM ONE (traditional bureaucracy)	CHAOS (caused by current changes)	FORM TWO (customer satisfaction)
Lots of paperwork	Lack of new job descriptions	More independence
Rigid hierarchy	Will I be laid off?	Customer-satisfaction surveys
Predictability	Conflicting technical systems	Employees evaluated on customer satisfaction

Prompt responses to customer questions ⟶

A typical "homework" list from our introductory session. Using the three-stage model of change as a template, employees listed elements of Form One (the old bureaucracy), Form Two (their visions of the revitalized organization), and Chaos (the phase most of them were presently in). They also circled those parts of the old form that could be preserved in the new one. The assignment was created primarily to get people to consider the personal impact of the agency's changes. We wanted them to consider exactly what they personally stood to gain and lose, and to identify chaotic elements—unanswered questions, hot spots of resistance, and other ongoing problems—that needed resolution.

The assignment's primary purpose was to get people to reflect. It asked them to look at the three stages of change in *personal* terms: What is the bureaucratic form like for *you*? What forms do you work with now? How is *your* work made turbulent, messy, or chaotic by the current changes? What do *you* envision in the new customer-oriented form? By answering these questions, employees started to determine what they stood to gain and lose by the change. They could see what they would have to give up, and what parts of their jobs they might hang on to.

There were a few beneficial side effects of the assignment. One was that it kept people moving forward. We had just uncorked a bottle of chaos, and while it's very important not to suppress chaos, it's equally important not to wallow in chaos. The assignment sent the message that because people were unhappy with the change, this wasn't an excuse for stagnation. The agency would still look to the future, and change would happen whether they came along or not. Another side effect was that labeling chaos and explaining it was normal reassured people. It helped them see chaos as a phase, not a permanent condition.

Debriefing

This first-day material boils down to a few key techniques. Essentially, what we did was to "contain the chaos." We didn't try to shut it down, nor did we let it run amok. We established clear parameters—a certain place at a certain time, with certain rules—within which chaos could surface. Chaos did surface: people spoke up, asked questions, complained, and even praised the changes. We affirmed their reactions, whatever the reactions were, then we moved on.

The container for the chaos—the "four walls"—was already in place when we started. When we entered the "arena," we performed three tasks:

> To "contain chaos," provide a safe place—an interim form—where chaos can surface and be resolved.

1. *We began building trust* by laying out the contract for safety.

2. *We provided facts and gathered questions.* An important fact we reiterated was the change was definitely going to happen and people needed to take it seriously.

3. *We dealt openly with people's reactions, and encouraged them to reflect on what the change meant to them personally.* Because we listened to people's questions and concerns, they were more willing to give the new forms a chance. This is in large part a matter of trust. When people see their concerns are recognized and valued, they begin to *feel* the safety built into the system. The more they trust, the more they're willing to engage in *shaping* the change.

Commitment is required in these initial sessions. When an organization faces the rampant bull of chaos, it's easy to just leave the arena, but the chaos can be tamed. In time, more people will come to trust the process. Soon they'll say, "I've got my questions answered well enough. My reactions are out and I've been heard. I know this change is going forward and I have to choose what I'm going to do." Chaos, however difficult to endure in the short term, is a crucial step toward that decisive moment.

Readiness

One further effect of the early sessions was to get people psychologically *ready* to see possibilities for the future. When people embark on change, chaos often stands in their way like a seven-foot-tall wrestler. They can't see anything but an intimidating hulk.

Confronted by this threat, baffled by the loss of familiar tools, people may see the future as dangerous or depressing. The early sessions help change that attitude. For one thing, people learn that the organization can and will go ahead—there's no retreating to worn-out ways. People also begin exploring the ways they personally can defeat the behemoth standing in their way.

> *In order to invest in change, people must be ready to look at the future. They must start to resolve unfinished business and get their questions answered.*

Think back to the story of the school principal. His holding onto a grudge for eight years was an example of *not being ready* to change. He couldn't envision a better future. All he could see was the past. Ironically, it was only when he reflected on and talked about the past that he became ready to help change the faculty contract and move the school ahead. Anyone can rise to the challenge as he did and clear a path toward a better future.

THE MIDDLE SESSIONS: MOVING THE VISION

The second and third sessions at the agency were heavy on practice. We assigned projects to get employees thinking about and practicing the customer satisfaction techniques developed by our colleagues at Public Strategies Group. We explained that by the last session, these projects would be fleshed out as "action plans" and actually implemented.

Much of our time was spent with facts: how to measure customer satisfaction and discover what customers really want. We presented this information in our own way. As we delved into these facts, we paid close attention to the reactions that surfaced. When people had questions and reactions, we used the opportunity to open a dialogue.

Dialogue

In chapter six, "Trust," and chapter seven, "Breakthrough Leadership," we talk about dialogue in detail—how to encourage, guide, and make it matter. Dialogue was a crucial component of all our workshops at the agency, too. Every time we introduced facts, we allowed people to ask questions and voice their reactions. Every time we asked people to reflect on their experience, we followed up the reflection with dialogue.

Dialogue connects the other three "clarifiers" of facts, reflection, and guidance (figure 5–2). Through dialogue, people can learn facts. They can talk about their experience and their reflections, and seek guidance.

Figure 5–2

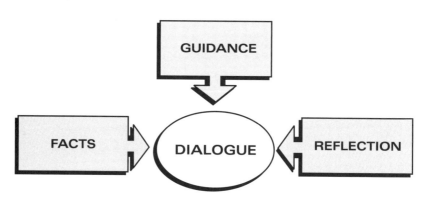

Dialogue is the meeting ground of facts, reflection, and guidance. Through dialogue, people learn facts, talk about their reflections, ask questions, and receive guidance.

Here's an example of how dialogue works, taken from one of the middle sessions. One of the most obdurate work units was from the travel audit office. These people processed travel reimbursement claims, and one of them, Yvette Gankin, was an outspoken critic of the training. She had proclaimed she would rather endure childbirth ten times than attend the workshops.

The story of the travel auditor's dialogue.

During one of the assignments, her unit's frustration boiled over. We had asked them to identify their customers—a necessary first step toward providing customer satisfaction. Some groups had some trouble with the assignment. (Writers in the publication unit had debated endlessly whether their customers were their bosses—the editors who put the brochures together—or the public, who read the brochures.) The travel auditors were particularly frustrated. They understood they had "internal" customers—every employee who submitted travel receipts—but insisted they already provided good service and didn't need to improve. "We're in touch with our customers all the time," they said. "We know what they want."

We were less certain. Saying that you're in touch with your customers is not valid data. The group's coach struggled to get them to do the exercise, and they resisted. "We're overwhelmed by work," they complained. "This training is only keeping us from doing our jobs." They refused to participate and spent their time gossiping about the office.

During a break, the coach asked us for help. This was a golden opportunity. Every participant in the room was a customer of the travel audit office. We could practice talking to customers about providing better service right now.

We told everyone we were going to do some intensive dialogue. We put the travel auditors at tables in front of the room and asked them to consult with the other participants, who were their customers.

They dove right in. The travel auditors explained the facts of the reimbursement process and described the constraints they worked under. Then their customers took their turn.

Most of the questions were specific and fact-oriented. "Why is this expense reimbursable, but that one's not?" The auditors were surprised that people didn't already know this stuff. Maybe their customers didn't understand the policies as well as they thought, and their service wasn't as top-notch as they boasted. The travel auditors answered every question patiently and thoroughly.

Other questions weren't so much about facts. They were really complaints and affected spirit. One man complained about a business trip he had taken. He had a reservation at a hotel that offered discounts to government employees, but when he arrived late, his room had been given out. He went to another hotel—one that didn't give the discount—and been forced to make up the difference out of his own pocket.

The auditors were distressed by such stories. Yvette, the "childbirth" woman, responded vigorously. "If that ever happens to you again," she said, "You call me anytime. I'll give you my home number and email, and I pledge I will help you twenty-four hours a day. We'll figure something out." Now *that* is customer service.

At the same time, Gankin and her colleagues had their own complaints about employees. "If you send me a reimbursement form and don't sign it," one travel auditor scolded, "there's nothing I can do but send it back."

This dialogue helped people see several things more clearly. They now knew the facts of the reimbursement process, and each side saw the efforts and the aggravations of the other. Most important, everyone in the room saw what the agency meant when it told them to work with their customers to provide greater satisfaction. They understood the *facts* and the *experience* of customer service. Most of the participants became converts; they personally understood and embraced the new forms.

Most remarkable was the transformation of Yvette Gankin. She seemed like a different person. No longer sitting with an expression of bored disdain, she looked vigorous, open, excited—the picture of vitality. When she saw how the new forms were supposed to work, she embraced them exuberantly. She even volunteered to coach in the next series of workshops. In the following months she became one of the most enthusiastic and effective advocates for change. This became possible thanks to dialogue.

Hers was not an isolated example. The woman who'd complained at the first session that she wanted to be left alone to "do her job" also became a coach. Not everyone bought in so enthusiastically, of course. Some individuals dug in and never budged. Some work units descended into chaos and looked as if they would never come out. Others put in minimal effort. Still, in every workshop we made progress. More people were coming around. Achieving critical mass throughout the organization looked possible.

Debriefing

What lesson can we draw from these "turning the corner" sessions? The most important is that *people began to see a clear vision of their personal place in the organization's future.* Clarification strives for this kind of insight.

The travel auditors embraced the changes because they discovered several things: what customer satisfaction really means, that new forms will make them more effective, and working this way will make their jobs more interesting. The change became both *real* and *appealing.*

They reached this understanding through a combination of fact-finding, reflection, dialogue, and guidance. *Facts* came when the travel auditors explained their systems, and when they learned about their customers' frustrations and confusion. *Reflection* took place as everyone in the room considered their experience of the travel audit procedures. *Dialogue* made these facts and experiences explicit. The dialogue resolved conflicts and answered questions, and put everyone on the same page. Our *guidance* set up the dialogue and encouraged people not to mistake personal assumptions for the truth.

> *The travel auditors understood how the new forms worked (events) and how the new forms would "feel" (experience). This understanding came from facts, reflection, dialogue, and guidance.*

The result was *clarity.* The workshop participants now understood the new forms *personally.*

The change was no longer transactional. Their spirits were involved. They sensed what the new, customer-satisfaction-driven agency would be like, and how they could help create their future.

At this point they could have said, "Forget it," and continued to resist the changes. They could have quit their jobs rather than change. We've seen it happen. Fortunately, Glenn and Baird had put forth a vision that was easy to buy into. The employees knew that the agency's new forms would reward their investments of spirit. They embraced the new forms, which moved the agency that much closer to achieving critical mass.

The most important thing to note is *clarity arrived when people had a personal experience of the new form.* At that moment, the administrators' vision moved out of the realm of abstract decree and into the employees' hearts and minds. The employees reached a *decisive moment*: they had to engage with the new forms or resist, but they could no longer be neutral.

> *When the auditors clearly understood the new forms, they faced a decisive moment. Would they invest in the new forms or reject them?*

THE LATER SESSIONS: ENGAGEMENT AND RESISTANCE

During the third and fourth workshops, participants split into three distinct groupings. The first group was the vanguard. Like the travel auditors, these people understood and embraced the new forms. They became enthusiastic leaders who tried to bring their colleagues along. The group in the middle went along, but didn't invest much spirit. Finally, there were the resisters, and they were as entrenched as ever.

Some of the most recalcitrant members of the agency were the middle managers, who had the most invested in the old forms. Unlike the top administrators, these managers had the new forms imposed on them. Unlike the rank and file, they had some power. The new system, which would make customer satisfaction central, looked like it would give some of that power to employees who were dealing directly with customers. Some managers saw the focus on customer satisfaction as a threat to their power, and sensed they were being given new responsibilities without getting any new authority.

While some managers resisted giving power to employees, others complained that their employees wouldn't *take* any power. "My people just won't go along with this," said one. Another griped, "My staff says this is all a waste of time. They refuse to do anything."

It was true that some employees did say these things. Moreover, the managers were in the difficult position of having to exhort their people to invest in changes when they were skeptical.

Not all the managers disliked the new forms, but a significant number did. To hear their concerns and try to get them to buy in, we hosted a workshop to provide extra help for them.

For a while, the workshop went quite badly. The managers recited their complaints. We listened, took notes, and tried to move on and discuss other things. A handful of agitators refused to cooperate, and kept raising objections and asking hostile questions. When we tried to get them to reflect on ways they could improve their situation, they simply refused. When we divided the participants into groups for dialogue, the agitators shot down all discussion with cynical, even cruel comments. They mocked anyone who tried to participate.

Though we recognized that almost all the managers distrusted the new forms, we also saw that most were willing to try the workshop. They needed reassurance, and to see there would be a payoff. The vocal protesters held the workshop hostage, especially the small groups.

We were fed up and put aside the regular agenda to draw a bell-curve on a whiteboard. We explained the goal of achieving critical mass—that you didn't need everyone to make a change stick. Then we issued a challenge: "Okay. You can't get everyone on your staff aboard. What are you going to do about it? You have a choice. You can give up and your unit will be left behind, or, if you want to move ahead, you need to work with the employees ready to get with the program. Don't waste your resources on the resisters. We're looking for critical mass, not universal buy-in."

This was really a bit of gamesmanship. We wanted to give the managers a way of dealing with intransigent employees, and their intransigent peers. By talking about critical mass, we sent a message to the workshop participants: they didn't need to let the vocal protesters shut down their agenda.

Luckily, the gambit worked. Several of the groups moved to isolate the resisters among them. They told the complainers to keep quiet or leave while they did their work. In this way, they began to solve their problems.

Debriefing

The resistance levied by the managers and travel auditors is common. Moving ahead inevitably means confronting honest, reasonable objections to change. Usually, groups that have trouble are willing to accept focused attention and help. Some refuse it and become active resisters and saboteurs.

Handling people who refuse to engage is an essential skill to master. Resistance happens everywhere, though some of the most savage resistance we've ever encountered, ironically enough, was at a pair of churches. We'll detour briefly from the agency's story to show how the churches overcame their resisters.

Facing Resistance: The Churches' Story

Two churches stood at opposite ends of a Minnesota farm town. Both were Catholic and founded by immigrant farmers a hundred years earlier. The difference was the south church was German, and the north church Czech. For their entire history the churches remained separate, competitive if not quite distrustful.

As in small towns all across America, the population was dwindling. Young people moved to Minneapolis rather than take on the headaches and uncertainty of modern farming. The population could no longer support two congregations. The bishop, along with the priest who served both churches, decided to combine them.

The backlash was swift and ferocious. How dare the bishop betray the farmers' heritage? How could the congregants be expected to give up a building they had been worshipping in for a century, in which the most significant moments of their lives—baptisms, weddings, funerals—had taken place? It would be a searing loss.

The local priest bore the brunt of the hostility. Though he took many of the steps we suggest—hosting open discussions, clarifying facts, listening and listening and listening—and though many of the congregants agreed with him, the resisters wouldn't budge. Several families stopped speaking to him. He received death threats. It got so bad that he asked the bishop for a transfer. Another priest, Father Fortin, replaced him.

On one of Fortin's first nights in town, the telephone woke him after midnight. The caller said, "If you close our church, we'll come over there and cut your balls off."

"I'm celibate," replied Fortin, unintimidated. "If you want 'em, come get 'em."

The Virtues of Transaction

How does an organization handle that kind of hostility? The best response is to disengage spirit, to become transactional.

Most of the Clarification process is an attempt to get everyone to engage with one another at the level of spirit. When one person or faction consistently refuses to invest spirit, the others have to protect themselves. In the same way you can't negotiate with terrorists, you can't simply march your own spirit into the open when the other party remains armed and entrenched. When one party in a dialogue won't engage spirit, the relationship must become formal and transactional.

> When one party in the Clarification process refuses to invest spirit, the relationship must become transactional.

There's no point in persisting to engage such people in a dialogue. For one thing, people like the midnight caller won't negotiate. Talking openly with them would be dangerous. Even when there's no physical threat, honest dialogue makes people vulnerable. You don't open up to those who won't respect your humanity.

This is ironic: *in order to have a reflective, spirited culture, the organization may have to deal with some of its own people in a transactional manner.*

Experienced leaders know this is a fact of life. You can't let fear, hostility, or cynicism hold your organization hostage. Make a good faith effort to give people what they need, then call the question and set a deadline after which you get on with business.

Figure 5–3

STEPS FOR DEALING WITH INTRANSIGENT RESISTERS

1. *Respect resistance and listen to it.* People often have very good reasons for disliking change.

2. *Provide focused attention* **and help** resolve particularly difficult conflicts.

3. *"Call the question."* If resisters don't move toward engaging in the process, it's time to set a deadline. If they won't engage, there will be consequences.

4. *Become transactional.* If the deadline isn't met—if there isn't honest movement toward conciliation—stop trying to engage. Follow whatever formal, fair procedures are necessary to isolate the resistance.

Father Fortin followed the steps in figure 5–3. At yet another meeting to discuss the plans, the discussion was shouted down by strident partisans. Father Fortin had finally had enough. He believed that most of the families were on his side and decided to bring the issue to a vote. The congregants filled out ballots and the church secretary tallied the results.

The vote to combine the churches won in a landslide. Fortin had expected to win, but not so handily—the passion of the resistance had disguised its weakness. In the following months, after an emotional ceremony in which the south church congregation celebrated its history and then paraded with its most treasured icons to the north church for a united Mass, a few of the hostile families returned to the fold while the others simply drifted away.

Fortin's patient explanation of facts and listening to people's reactions had built critical mass. With that critical mass, he was able to defeat the resisters and make their hostility irrelevant.

THE FINAL SESSION

Back at the agency, more groups and individuals were embracing the change. They readied their customer-service action plans for presentation on the final day. People asked technical questions about the process and fine-tuned their ideas. They put slide shows together and rehearsed their talks.

When they gave their presentations, a member of the senior administrative team—usually Nancy Baird, but often Eugene Glenn—attended. A few of the presentations were scattershot or half-hearted, but most employees did a professional job. Some were giddy with pride. We had to be rigorous in our time-keeping, because they wanted to go on.

Finally, Glenn and Baird joined in a debriefing of the entire training. They sat in a "fishbowl" surrounded by the participants and answered questions. (Our only rule was, "Be respectful." People were.)

This crucial event was the first time many of the employees had ever met the agency chiefs, much less conversed with them. This was a strong show of support from the top. Even more important, the "fishbowls" became real dialogues. Glenn and Baird didn't wait for questions. They asked their own and sought input and advice. What worked in these sessions? What didn't? How can we help you implement your action plans? What confuses you? Far from being defensive, they were open, confident, and honest. They made sure they understood what the employees were saying. When they didn't have an answer, they admitted it. They confessed they were often confused themselves. At the same time, they unequivocally repeated the message that the transformation would go forward.

Debriefing

The events at the agency were a success, but this was not nearly the end of the job. By the last session, most employees voiced willingness to try the new forms. Many new forms still had to be created and installed. There would be a lot of questions and problems in the future; real trust was only beginning to take hold. The agency had to institutionalize these changes.

Ironically, one of the immediate challenges facing the agency—and other organizations that ignite people's spirits—was dealing with all the enthusiasm. The energy of the employees who "got it" was astounding. New ideas ricocheted around the agency like popcorn. The agency had passed a point of no return. People *demanded* to be involved in the change.

POSTSCRIPT: FINDING A VISION (or, What to Do When You Don't Know What to Do Next)

In the past two chapters, we have described how Clarification helped the agency transform itself. What happens when an organization needs to change and doesn't *have* a vision of the future? What happens when no one really knows what to do next? When the organization is stuck?

Consider the suburban church that lost its dynamic pastor in chapter two, "Form and Spirit's Difficult Road." Before that loss, the church had followed the pastor's vision. When the pastor left, his vision seemed impossible to achieve. The church leadership needed to develop a new vision to guide it.

Consider what happens when an organization grows so rapidly that it plunges into chaos. In our stories of the bank and the university, we saw how success can turn into mayhem. Those institutions found they needed to re-evaluate their visions.

It is easy to slide into chaos. It is extremely difficult to find the path back out. Much of our work is with clients who don't know what comes next. Some have endured a tough random change. Others want to make a developmental change, but don't know what the next step should be. Still others blinked once and found the world had changed—they need to figure out where they are and what to do next. *Implementing* a vision, as the agency was doing, must wait. The most pressing need is to *develop* a vision.

What distinguishes implementing a vision from developing one? In both cases, we use Clarification. We bring people together in interim forms with the "four walls" of safety, time, space apart, and other resources. Within the four walls, we use the "clarifiers" of facts, personal reflection, dialogue, and guidance. We work through events and experience until the group achieves clarity—in this case, about where the organization needs to go.

The crucial difference is in *what questions you ask to spark reflection and dialogue*. At the agency, the reflection and dialogue were all about adapting to a new situation. When you're searching for a vision, the reflection and dialogue are all about *creating* a new situation.

At an organization like the suburban church or the university, leaders tried to figure out what to do next. They needed to invent new forms that sustained spirit, and didn't know what those forms would be. They couldn't even say for sure where the organization's spirit was, or what it needed.

> *To find a vision, as opposed to implementing one, is also a matter of Clarification. The difference is in the questions you ask when gathering facts, reflecting, and engaging in dialogue.*

In such a situation, we recommend the following "clarifying questions." Leaders should ask these questions—through questionnaires, interviews, "speaking circles," workshops, or any other forum—of as many people as possible.

FOUR QUESTIONS TO HELP CLARIFY A VISION

1. "What are the facts of the current situation, as you understand them?"

This question serves two related purposes. First, it gathers facts. It tells you what people know, and reveals facts you didn't know. Second, it identifies the places where facts aren't clear. People could have their facts wrong, or there could be gaps in their knowledge. Asking this question allows you to learn facts, figure out which facts need to be clearer, and helps you answer questions and misunderstandings. All of this establishes the "fact" side of Clarification.

2. "What is your experience of the current situation?"

This was a question we asked in the university's "speaking circles," described in chapter three, "Three Principles of Vitality." The question allows people to voice their opinions, vent emotions, and put unfinished business on the table. It *gets people to reflect on and talk about their place in the organization.* That's a critical step in creating one-person-at-a-time organizational change.

3. "Where would you like to see the organization go in the future?"

This question is designed to get people brainstorming and dreaming about possibilities. It is a *spirit* question. What it really asks is, "what does your spirit want from this organization?" Because this question is about the future, it's a natural follow-up to the previous question, which asks people about the present.

4. "What structures would make it possible to turn this vision into reality?"

The previous question was about spirit; this one is about form. In the previous question, we ask people what their spirits want. Here we ask them what forms their spirits would fit into.

It's important to ask about spirit first. We don't want people thinking only about form. When people think about possible forms *before* they consider what their spirits want, they often think too small. Their imagination is limited. We ask them to "think with their spirits" before they even begin to consider forms. It is much better to search for forms that will fit spirit, rather than trying to fit spirit into next available form.

These questions provide a lot of information crucial for making decisions. For example, they tell leaders how much information their people have, identify and resolve current conflicts and unfinished business, and can generate fresh ideas and visions for the future.

What's more, answering these questions *gets people engaged.* In chapter three, the story of the university and its "speaking circles," showed that the more people had a voice in university policy, the more they invested spirit into the school's forms. By asking people where they're at and where they want the organization to go, leaders begin to get them invested in change. They move them toward critical mass: people begin to push for change even before the new forms are visible. Once the organization

CLARIFYING QUESTIONS

For finding a vision

1. "What are the facts of the current situation, as you understand them?"

2. "What is your experience of the current situation?"

3. "Where would you like to see the organization go in the future?"

4. "What structures would make it possible to turn this vision into reality?"

decides which vision to implement, the battle to overcome resistance and apathy is already partly won.

SUMMARY

During the agency's Clarification workshops, we saw a pattern. Most people would enter the first session hostile, cynical, or anxious. Our effort went into making them feel safe and helping them understand what was going on.

Over the series of workshops, they began to understand what the new forms were going to look like. They had opportunities to "practice" with these forms in the assignments we gave them and workshop dialogues.

Some people embraced these new forms right away. Others went along for the ride—becoming involved but not particularly committed or identified with the idea of giving great customer service—and others fought tooth and nail. The agency did finally build a critical mass of engagement and the changes went through with enough people invested in the new customer satisfaction model to make it work.

This general pattern, from suspicion to acceptance, repeated itself at the agency. This is the pattern of change: suspicion, distrust, fear, and anger are part of chaos. Leaders who want to transform their organization should remember this pattern. They need to be patient and remember that change will plunge the organization and its people into chaos. Interim forms and Clarification can "contain the chaos," making it manageable, but it's chaos nonetheless. People need safety, time, space, and other resources you get through chaos. They need facts, time for reflection and dialogue, and able guidance. When leaders provide these "four walls" and "four clarifiers," the organization will thrive even during enormous change.

VI * TRUST

or a long time, we saw trust as an auxiliary to change. We were interested in trust and safety insofar as they helped people reach clarity. It was only later we began to see trust as vitality's central determining factor. Without trust, there can be no vitality.

FORM, SPIRIT, AND TRUST

It's impossible to understand form and spirit—and therefore vitality—without understanding their connection to trust. Trust is implicit any time a person invests spirit in form. You have to trust a form to engage with it. The more people trust a form, the deeper they invest spirit. If they don't trust it, they'll protect their spirits by resisting engagement.

This phenomenon had a major impact on our work at the agency. During our early workshops, agency employees didn't trust much. They didn't trust their bosses, the customer-service initiative, and our workshop. Until they began to trust, they weren't going to invest any spirit into these forms. That's why we spent so much time trying to help them feel safe. Without their spirits, our forms were useless.

Trust was also a core issue for the bank presidents, who endured dreadful meetings because they believed they couldn't ask questions and criticize. They didn't trust they could be themselves. The truth wasn't welcome at their meetings.

Trust is important in how people invest in forms and each other. The school principal came to hate his faculty because they boycotted his barbecue. They had broken his trust. Meanwhile, the teachers hadn't trusted him. After he confessed that he had withdrawn his spirit from the school, the teachers apologized to him. Then they told their side of the story.

When the principal invited people to his party, the teachers were holding out for better terms on their contract. They didn't see his invitation as an effort to help everyone get along. They saw it as an effort to soften the union, to divide and conquer during negotiations. The teachers believed the invitations had been given in bad faith. They hadn't trusted the principal.

Now the principal saw his own complicity in the conflict. He had been naïve and failed to look at things from the teachers' point of view. With neither side trusting the other, they all disengaged from the relationship. During our workshop eight years later, they finally talked about this mutual distrust and realized their distrust had been misplaced. The principal understood why the teachers had not come to the party. The teachers understood he hadn't been trying to undercut them. They set aside their distrust and began to rebuild their relationship.

Trust is a major component of our daily work. Sometimes we build trust during change workshops; we also do specific, trust-building projects. One of the biggest of these was a program to make trust part of the corporate culture at a Fortune 500 company.

The company saw a direct correlation between trust and innovation. Distrust made people afraid to question assumptions and propose risky ideas.

The company hired us because of employees' surprising responses to a survey about their work lives. Much to management's surprise, the survey revealed low morale and dismal levels of trust in a major division. Employees in the division believed any mistake could derail their careers. They kept their opinions and creative ideas to themselves, fearing that if they questioned a boss's decision or their idea failed, they would be professionally destroyed.

The revelations were particularly surprising since this company prided itself on innovation and trust. It manufactured household and industrial materials, and invented a number of products that changed the marketplace. In a fiercely competitive environment, the company had always been a leader in innovation. Moreover, the company strove to never lay off an employee. Its benefits and community service were legendary, and the company prided itself on being a trustworthy part of people's lives.

The survey showed that in this division, the company was failing to live up to its ideals. Employees might trust they would be taken care of, but their fear of saying or doing the wrong thing kept them from investing fully in their work. Management realized this was dampening their creativity. If people were afraid to tell the truth or venture a risky idea, they wouldn't generate the environment of experimentation so crucial to innovation.

We spent four years building trust within the company. During that time, we found ample evidence of the importance of trust to vitality and success.

On our first day, we asked workshop participants to think of someone they trusted. Then we asked, "What is it about that person that inspires your trust?" and, "What impact does that have on you?"

Unlike employees at the agency, people here were excited to talk. What made someone trustworthy? "They're dependable." "They're open." "They're not judgmental." "They show up and pay attention when you're talking." "They tell the truth."

Even more compelling were the effects of trust. "When I'm trusted, I can be myself," people said. "I don't have to be on stage." "I can take risks and make mistakes." "I can ask questions."

"We have trust in our unit," someone said, "and it makes things fun. We laugh a lot."

"I work harder for people who trust me," said somebody else. "I don't want to let them down. When I get micro-managed by someone who doesn't trust me to do my own job, I just do the bare minimum."

We followed up this discussion by asking them to think of someone they *dis*trusted.

What made someone untrustworthy? "They don't keep their promises." "They tell me one thing, then tell somebody else the opposite." "They don't say what they really think." "They talk about people behind their backs." "They don't trust me." "When you try to give them constructive criticism, they dodge responsibility. I don't trust anyone who can't admit a mistake."

> One person observed that "when you spend a lot of time around someone you don't trust, you can become untrustworthy yourself."

One woman said, "I had a supervisor who was too nice. She gave me all kinds of praise, but I never trusted her because she never criticized me, even when we both knew I'd messed up."

Distrust damages morale. As distrust grows, people tend to protect themselves from one another. They don't bring out their best ideas and become self-protective rather than collaborative. Suspicion blossoms. People attribute the worst motives to each other. One person told us, "Our relationship with management is so bad right now that even when they're being trustworthy, we'd rather believe rumors than what they're saying." Another added, "When you spend a lot of time around someone you don't trust, you can become untrustworthy yourself. You begin to avoid that person, and complain about them behind their back. You don't tell people what you're thinking and you resist cooperation. You essentially freeze that person out, and suddenly find you're contributing to a really poisonous atmosphere."

As we continued to explore how trust works, we established a list of several "Markers of Trust." These indicators can help people identify the symptoms brought on by trust and distrust (figure 6–1).

TWO TRUTHS ABOUT TRUST

The lesson of these markers of trust is the degree to which trust affects vitality. Trust makes it possible for spirit to blossom. Distrust is the quickest path to superficial relationships and a transactional culture.

The contrast between trust and distrust in the division was so stark that literally everyone in the workshops saw the value of making trust a priority. Trust was good for the organization—and good for individuals. Trust enhances creativity and experimentation, and makes everyone's day-to-day work life more enjoyable and meaningful.

Two facts about trust are particularly relevant here:

1. *Trust is not "soft."* On the contrary, this is one of the hardest things an organization can take on—both in the sense it is hard to do, and has hard, bottom-line consequences. Among other things, trust requires fairness, excellent communication, diligence, a willingness to put oneself in another's shoes, and the strength to resolve conflict directly rather than

Figure 6–1

MARKERS OF TRUST	MARKERS OF DISTRUST
Being "real" is more important than looking good.	Appearance is everything. People tend to say, "I can't be myself."
People confront problems directly and respectfully.	Conflicts are allowed to fester, or there is "triangulation" in which people complain about each other to third parties.
Respect shown for those who aren't present.	Gossip, rumors, back-biting.
Privacy respected.	Secrecy is prized. People maintain power by withholding information.
People say what must be said.	There are "undiscussable" subjects no one will talk about.
People accept personal responsibility.	People shift blame away from themselves.
Efficiency. People are trusted to do their work. Problems are addressed and resolved directly.	Inefficiency and redundancy. One manager said, "We spend millions on distrust—we have third-party reviews, forms to fill out, second-guessing, and constant revision."
Teamwork.	Turf battles.
It's okay to ask questions and acknowledge not knowing how to do something.	Facade of perfection and perfect knowledge.
Mistakes are seen as opportunities for learning.	Mistakes occasion retribution.
Differentiation and diversity.	Uniformity. People stifle their individuality to fit in. Example: a pair of teachers who won national awards didn't tell anyone in their school for fear they would be labeled as arrogant.
People's reservations are honored. If someone has misgivings about an idea, they are invited to speak about them.	Blind loyalty.
Spirited rituals bring the community together (for anniversaries, achievements, and personal milestones).	There are no rituals or celebrations, or they are done by rote.
Humor, fun.	Over-seriousness and fear.
People express a range of emotions from excitement to despair.	Limited, controlled emotion.

let it fester. Its effect on the bottom line is evidenced by the fact that this company was willing to invest four years and a lot of money to build trust into its corporate structure.

2. *Trust is not about getting everyone to like each other and wear a happy face.* One of the more surprising truths about trust is that *you can trust someone you don't like and you can like someone you don't trust.* When Mary served on city council, she didn't particularly like a couple of her colleagues—but their word was good and they performed their jobs with integrity and good will. At the same time, one of the more affable, likeable council members voted capriciously and often failed to meet commitments he'd made. Trust isn't only about liking people. It's about honesty, fairness, and mutual respect. Being honest and fair means that not every situation will be full of laughs. It sometimes means being contentious and exasperated. Trust demands being *engaged*—telling the truth and sticking with a demanding process—even when pretending everything is just fine might be easier.

> *TWO TRUTHS ABOUT TRUST*
>
> *1. Trust is not "soft."*
>
> *2. Trust is not about getting everyone to like one another.*

WHAT IS TRUST?

This anecdote is a good metaphor for trust. One day, Chuck went to buy some flowers for Mary. As the florist wrapped the roses, she said, "Be sure to put the flowers in warm water."

"Warm water? Why?"

"If you put them in warm water, the blossoms open. If you put them in cold water, they stay closed."

Trust is like warm water. If you put people in a warm, trustworthy environment, they tend to bloom. In a cold, untrustworthy environment, people clamp shut.

To return to the language of form and spirit: spirit blossoms when nurtured by trust-friendly forms. When people feel secure in a form, they express themselves honestly. They invest spirit.

We call this *a felt sense of safety*. Earlier, when we talked about the importance of safety in Clarification, we observed that people could be safe but not actually *feel* safe. Remember the agency employees who fretted because they saw somebody taking photos near our workshop? They were safe, but they didn't feel safe, and so withheld their trust.

> *We define trust as "a felt sense of safety."*

Similarly, recall the woman who complained that after a few months in the transactional culture of her office, she no longer felt like a hundred-watt light bulb, but like a twenty-watt bulb that only flickered on occasionally. She worked in a "cold-water" environment. She couldn't trust that her good ideas would be taken seriously. She couldn't even trust she could be herself: she had to hide her light under a bushel basket.

The first order of business when you're trying to build trust is to ensure people feel that they're in "warm" forms—or among "warm" people—that will keep them safe. The four walls of Clarification go a long way toward providing safety. Space apart, for instance, can signal to people that they are in a refuge.

What else do people need to begin to trust? The most important prerequisite to trust is trust. Someone has to make a first gesture.

THE CONTRACT FOR SAFETY

The "contract for safety" is our own first trust gesture. We use this contract to launch all our workshops. At the agency, we promised that we held what people said in confidence: we might tell the administrators what we had been told, but only in general terms and never attribute a particular statement to a particular person or group. We also promised to hear and respect all opinions and get answers to people's questions, and asked the participants to abide by the same rules.

The "contract for safety" makes Clarification possible. Even if work-

shop participants aren't positive they are safe to speak openly, the contract provides enough safety for them to try. They trust a little, and invest
a little spirit. When they see we're serious about the contract, they trust a
little more. They invest more in the process.

Just as trust is essential for Clarification, so Clarification builds
trust (see figure 6–2). The more people engage in Clarification, the
more they trust one another. Like the bank presidents, they begin to tell
the truth. Like the bank's auditors, they begin to understand their colleagues' experiences.

Figure 6–2

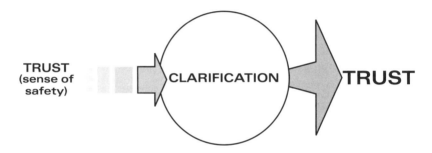

Just as you need trust for Clarification, so Clarification builds trust.

In a change workshop like the agency's, we lay out a contract for
safety and ask people to abide by it. The contract gives trust a jump-start,
then it can grow on its own. During a workshop specifically to build trust,
we don't just tell people to abide by a contract for safety. Instead, we have
participants work together to create a contract of their own.

At the company, we led dozens of small groups through trust-building
workshops. Each time we began a new set of workshops, the group spent
most of the first session establishing its own contract for safety.

We asked the participants to develop guidelines for their own workshop, and gave them suggestions. For instance, we told them people usually feel safer when they know what's said in the room stays in the room.
Many groups, especially those with both managers and regular employees
present, made agreements about reprisals. The managers promise not to

take revenge for something a staff member might say, and the staffers promise not to wage their own reprisals through gossip or reports to the union. While we made such suggestions, it was up to the group to negotiate its own contract.

In a trust-building workshop, participants establish their own contract for safety.

When a group creates a contract for safety, the important thing is not so much *what* the group includes, but *how* the decision is made. Some groups see speaking courteously as a fundamental issue. For others, courtesy isn't so important—they can be blunt without hurting trust. Both contracts are fine. What matters is that *successful groups give everyone a voice in writing a contract for safety.* There are all kinds of techniques to ensure that everyone's voice is heard, but they're beyond our scope here. Getting a good facilitator is highly recommended. Facilitators know how to help a group reach consensus and ensure that reticent participants get their say.

We've reproduced a contract for safety below, along with some explanatory footnotes.

ONE GROUP'S CONTRACT FOR SAFETY

We agree that we will...

1. *Maintain one another's anonymity.* We may talk to outsiders in general about our discussions, but we will not "quote" anyone or otherwise reveal particular identities.

2. *Listen with an open mind to others, and ask them to clarify what they say until we fully understand them.*

3. *Actively and respectfully participate in discussions.*[1]

4. *Take responsibility for our own role in the group's success. This means we will:*

- ask questions if we are confused

- listen to our own "feathers" of insight, inspiration, and reactions.

- bring any problems we have with the group to the group.[2]

- speak from our own experience, avoiding generalizations and abstractions.

5. *Avoid "triangulation."* If we have a conflict with another person, we will go to that person and resolve it. We will not triangulate by complaining or gossiping behind that person's back.

6. *Respect those who are not present.* We will not gang up on people who cannot hear what we're saying or defend themselves. We will not speak for them or quote them in their absence because of the danger of misinterpretation.

7. *Not wage reprisals* against group members for what they say.

8. *Respect and try to understand one another's "experiential worlds."* [3] People have a right to be who they are and to think and feel as they do. We will not try to force anyone to change.

9. *Be receptive to constructive criticism.*

10. *Not allow our roles to become barriers to communication.* Teamwork depends on a level playing field where each person can be heard, regardless of title, position, or experience.

NOTES

1. Active participation is as important as respectful participation. This is because withdrawing from dialogue is itself disrespectful, but more important, withdrawal can be a power play that disrupts dialogue.

2. Many times people withdraw from dialogue because they feel their voices aren't being heard or because they don't like the way the group is operating. On such occasions, it is the group member's responsibility to bring these problems into the open. It is not fair or productive for the member to withdraw and sulk. At the same time, it can be extremely difficult for an individual to feel safe enough to speak in such a situation. A facilitator will ensure this happens, and that the group takes his or her statements seriously.

3. See below for an explanation of "experiential worlds."

By writing its own contract for safety, a group will…

- Build its own "wall" of safety. This will facilitate Clarification.
- Begin to build trust by working together. Participants think and talk about what they need to feel safe, and as they do, they begin to feel safe with the group.
- Practice the art of trustworthy negotiation.

The contract for safety *does not need to be limited to Clarification workshops*. The terms of a contract for safety can and should apply to daily work. Any organization that establishes a contract for safety as an expectation for all its members, all the time, will go a long way toward creating a "warm water" environment where trust can blossom. Many of the groups we've worked with have maintained their contract for safety long after we departed.

> *A contract for safety can be used in daily work, not just Clarification. Every organization should establish its own contract for safety as a basic daily practice.*

USING CLARIFICATION TO BUILD TRUST

Trust is essential for Clarification and Clarification leads in turn to greater trust, but how exactly does this happen? What facts do you gather to build trust? What do you reflect on and talk about?

If you're coping with change as the agency was, then change is the topic of your Clarification. Trust will arise as a natural by-product of the process. If you are engaged in conflict resolution or team-building, then we recommend focusing on two items: *unfinished business* and *undiscussables*. These are focal points of trust, places where trust is built and broken. Even the most spirited, vitalized organizations need to address them. In the next sections, we describe these focal points, then offer a few tools to deal with them.

Trust Focal Point One: Unfinished Business

Unfinished business is unresolved conflict or pain. We once facilitated a trust-building exercise in a company where conflict between union and management had been fierce for years. It got so bad that people disregarded simple civility. During one session, a union representative told a supervisor, "I'd love to smash your face."

As we probed for the source of this animosity, people told us that "it all began twenty years ago," during a strike. The strike had ended and several contracts had been negotiated in the meantime, but the bad blood from those days had never stopped boiling. Back then, workers complained that managers were arrogant and abusive. Managers received threats at home.

> **FOCAL POINTS OF TRUST**
>
> *Unfinished business*
>
> *Undiscussables*

Each felt they were victimized and neither would apologize. The unfinished business of the strike festered like an infected wound. It would be nice to say that this example is unusual—that people who see each other every day don't hold twenty-year grudges—but a glance at any newspaper proves how common it is.

Unfinished business can result from any number of unresolved problems, such as:

- *Failure*. It can be very difficult for a company, for instance, to regain its confidence after a major product line fails.

- *Unmet expectations and unkept promises*. People who expect but don't receive a promotion, a raise, or any number of other benefits, can work over their grievance like a sore tooth, hating and savoring the pain.

- *Conflict*. Like the union/management conflict, many organizational battles can be fought repeatedly. Sometimes people just refuse to bury the hatchet, even when their anger and the conflict are no longer relevant or even helpful.

- *Misunderstandings that do not get clarified.* When one person misinterprets someone else, or hears a rumor about what another person said, people may assume the worst about another, but never directly address the issue.

- *Betrayal.*

All of these problems, from conflict to misunderstandings to betrayal, will hurt feelings. Once hurt, people curl up like flowers in cold water. The pain is often significant enough that it's just not worth repairing the damage and rebuilding trust.

Unfinished business remains unfinished because people don't want to open old, painful wounds. They would rather withdraw and hang on to their pain and anger. It is for this reason that we say *trust dies a quiet death*. People don't announce they have stopped trusting. To make such an announcement is to stay engaged, and be vulnerable again. Instead, when people stop trusting, they withdraw their spirits into themselves like turtles taking shelter in their shells.

Trust Focal Point Two: Undiscussables

Undiscussables are an organization's taboos, the things no one mentions. They are the proverbial 800-pound gorillas that everyone pretends are not in the room.

Once we were worked with a group of city employees, and had a hard time getting them to speak openly. People who worked side by side for years were measuring every word carefully. They were so polite it seemed they would shatter from the strain. We asked, "What's going on here you can't talk about? What are the undiscussable problems in your group?"

"Race," someone said without hesitation. Everyone nodded.

"Tell us about that. Why is it undiscussable?"

Suddenly the atmosphere in the room relaxed. Ironically, discussing the undiscussable was a relief. (It doesn't always work that way, but if the environment is a safe one, people generally can have a productive dialogue about undiscussables.)

A measure of the group's success came about half an hour later. One of the participants, a woman who left for an emergency meeting earlier in the day, returned. After listening a few minutes, she interrupted the conversation to ask, "Can I get caught up here? When I left, the conversation was really dragging, and now there's all this energy." She asked, "What did I miss?"

"We were talking about race," someone replied.

"Really?" she asked, shocked. "If we can talk about race, we can talk about anything."

Undiscussable subjects vary from one organization to the next, but they tend to concentrate in a few areas:

- *Race.* Race is America's national undiscussable. Despite the media attention race receives, it can be very difficult for people of different races—whites and blacks in particular—to speak frankly about their experience of race.

- *Gender issues.* This includes everything from sexual harassment to balancing work and home life.

- *Power*, particularly when it is being abused. When a boss rules imperiously, people cannot speak about it for fear of losing their jobs. When a colleague bullies, they tend to clam up out of intimidation.

- *Criticism* is often a taboo. This can occur when an organization is driven by conformity and people aren't allowed to question their bosses' decisions. Conformity can also be a trait of organizations that are "too nice." Everyone has encountered people or organizations where never is heard a discouraging word. For them, getting along is more important than getting ahead—but they get along to a fault. Workers smile at managers' bad decisions. Managers let low-performing employees slide by. No one has a complaint, but beneath the smiling exterior, people seethe with things they believe they cannot say. In such organizations, the *form* of Getting-Along, hollow as it is, becomes more important than the dynamic, often messy *spirit* of vitality.

Getting Along may be the primary motivation for keeping *any* subject undiscussable. It's hard to talk about race. It's scary to voice opinions that might get you labeled sexist. It's dangerous to complain about power-abuse. Bringing undiscussables into the open is often a relief; it's also likely to spark chaos.

Trust depends on truth. You can't be "real" with someone when you both refuse to acknowledge the 800-pound gorilla standing on the conference table.

CLARIFICATION: TOOLS FOR BUILDING TRUST

The focal points of trust—unfinished business and undiscussables—are "hot spots." They burn silently inside organizations, with everyone afraid to touch them.

Clarification is an effective tool for resolving unfinished business and airing undiscussables. Clarification creates a safe environment that minimizes the destructive force of these hot spots. Writing a contract for safety can prepare people to deal constructively with tough issues, and the guidance of a skilled facilitator can keep reflection and dialogue from devolving into a chaotic fight.

Within the "four walls" of Clarification, two techniques focus the fact-finding, reflection, and dialogue particularly well. They are excellent at building trust because they reveal unfinished business and undiscussables, and help clear out the conflict they cause.

> *CLARIFICATION TECHNIQUES FOR BUILDING TRUST*
>
> *Recapitulation*
>
> *Understanding experiential worlds*

Recapitulation

To recapitulate is to go back over something. We've found recapitulation the most effective tool for understanding and resolving conflict.

Recapitulation led the school principal to his confession about withdrawing his spirit. Each member of that trust-building workshop told his or her own story of the conflict from the beginning. The principal told the story of his barbecue. The teachers told their version of the story. When the truth came out, they understood one another and put the past behind them.

Another example is the high-tech plant that shut down. The scientists at the plant weren't immersed in conflict with each other, but still had suffered a hard blow. By telling their stories, they were able to distill the meaning of their experience. Their deepest trauma wasn't losing the job or income, it was uprooting their families again. Once these emotions were out in the open, people could deal with them directly, and then focus on the future.

Recapitulation—reviewing the history of something—excavates unfinished business. It builds trust by helping people understand themselves, their situation, and one another.

By recapitulating, you temporarily focus on the past, *before* considering the future. This relieves some of the pressure to rush toward a decision. You clarify how you got where you are, notice the moments when you lost your way or when conflict flared up, and identify crucial decisions. You remember guiding principles or core values that may have been dropped by the roadside.

Recapitulation builds trust for several reasons. First, it helps people understand the full story. All too often, people believe *their* understanding of history is the *only* one. The principal believed the union members were out to get him, while the teachers thought he'd been trying to undercut their unity. Each side had been well-intentioned, but each attributed evil motives to the other. The recapitulation revealed their errors.

The second reason recapitulation is effective is that it is the quickest way to expose and resolve unfinished business. People know—because they've often been brooding on it for years—what key moment led to conflict or a breakdown of trust. By recapitulating, they get to return to the key moment.

Our method is to set up a safe environment where people can simply tell their stories. Everybody gets to tell their story without being interrupted, and the others need to listen to the story *as that person's story*, not as that person's argument. It's not fair to argue over whether somebody's personal story is "correct" or not. The others will have turns to tell their own stories later, and they're welcome to provide their own interpretations of events at that time. *Everyone* gets to describe their own key moments and get them off their backs.

Finally, recapitulation can put undiscussables on the table. When people tell their stories honestly in a safe environment, issues like race, gender, power, and betrayal often arise. For example, someone might tell a story in which they feel one-down because they are black or a woman. Now the undiscussable is in the open—but it's in the open in a concrete, specific way. People aren't talking about "Race" or "Gender," they're talking about Cliff or Margaret's particular experience. A workshop can't solve the big issues of racism or sexism, but it can address particular incidents of racism, sexism, or other undiscussable problems.

To encourage a productive recapitulation, we ask people to reflect on a few questions on their own. For instance:

- What is the unfinished business in your own relationship with the organization and your colleagues?
- What were some of the key events that led the organization to this point?
- When did these problems begin?

Once people have a chance to think about these questions, they're better prepared to talk about them in a group. We always make sure that everyone in the group gets equal time to tell his or her story.

Understanding Experiential Worlds

Each person has his or her own "experiential world." By that term, we mean the way a person looks at the world—how their experiences shape the way they see things. The principal felt he'd been betrayed; in his "experiential world," he was a victim of cold-hearted teachers. In the teachers' "experiential world," he was out to destroy their unity and diminish their livelihood.

> Understanding some else's "experiential world" is the same as walking a mile in their shoes.

Understanding someone else's experiential world is the same as walking a mile in their shoes. This goes a long way toward building trust. Once the principal and the union leaders understood one another "from the inside," they resolved their conflict and restored trust. In the same way, our trust-building workshops at the Fortune 500 company were designed in part to get people to understand one another's experiential worlds. As participants told their own trust stories and understood the experiences of others, they also understood the company's trust situation more fully, and began to trust one another.

This is very much like the work we do on change. At the government agency, we wanted people to understand the change from the inside. Here in the trust workshops, we wanted people to understand trust from the inside. Along the way, they would come to understand *one another* from the inside.

Recapitulation and exploring experiential worlds can bring a group to clarity. Usually, when people understand their own stories in relation to others', they spontaneously trust more. This is not always the case. Clarification alone doesn't create trust. It gets people to the point where they can *choose* whether to trust.

At the government agency, Clarification helped people understand the changes around them. Once they understood, each person had to decide whether to invest spirit in the new forms or disengage. With trust, it's the same. You can understand another person's experiential world and their version of events, and still decide not to trust them. Sometimes, knowing all those things makes you trust somebody even less.

THE PARADOX OF TRUST AND RISK

Trust is a precursor to risk. People need to feel safe if they're going to risk speaking the truth, but no matter how much safety you have, trust is also always about risk. Even colleagues who trust each other take risks—they tell each other the painful truth when they have to, suggest new ideas their colleagues might hate, and fight out differences of opinion. Entire organizations take similar risks—for instance, altering a trusted product that no longer works in its old form.

Earlier we observed that trust is a prerequisite to trust. In order to build trust, someone has to take a risk and begin trusting. In truth, this process *never ends*. The first act of trust begets a second act of trust, which begets a third act, and on and on.

Trust is not static; it is a process. It grows or dies.

Trust doesn't mean that every risk will succeed. On the contrary, many risks can still end in failure; the risk-taker may look foolish or foolhardy and there may still be conflict and disagreement. Trust says it's okay to fail on the way to success, to look foolish on the way to new ideas, and that humans can disagree without destroying a relationship.

Here is another way to think about trust. In an atmosphere of distrust, speaking the truth and being yourself is dangerous. In a trusting relationship, the real risk is *not* to be "real" and speak the truth.

Trust means you continue to engage. The risk you take may fail, but don't give up. Someone may hurt you accidentally or even on purpose, but *if you have trust*, you don't give up on the person. You stick with the relationship and work it out.

> *In a trusting relationship,* *you* stay engaged. *Mistakes, conflicts, and problems are part of all relationships; with trust, they do not destroy the relationship.*

This is how to resolve the paradox of trust and risk. Trust creates safety and allows you to risk. Risk sets safety aside. Trust also means that even if you fail, you stick with the process, and keep your engagement with the form or the person.

SUMMARY

The impact of trust—and distrust—on vitality is complex and deep. An organization built on a foundation of trust is more likely to weather change, foster innovation, and resolve conflict. In a climate of distrust, people end up living lies. They cannot be themselves. They do not put their best ideas forward. They are not fully honest.

By using Clarification to recapitulate events and explore people's experiential worlds, an organization can go a long way toward building trust. Our experience has shown that when people work together in a civilized manner, when they reflect on their own thoughts and behavior and speak honestly from their own experience, they understand themselves and one another better. This understanding becomes the basis for authentic trust.

In this way, trust and vitality are within the grasp of those who reach for it.

VII ∗ BREAKTHROUGH LEADERSHIP

(or, What Do You Do Next?)

hat can you do personally to improve the vitality in your own life and organization? Regardless of your position in an organization, you have the power to influence vitality. The people who accept the challenge of improving vitality—of engaging spirit and building new forms—are the people who become leaders.

When we think of leaders, we often think of people who hold positions of authority: managers, presidents, and ministers. While true leaders fill many of these roles, they are only the *forms* of leadership. Holding a position of power does not automatically make one a leader. There are inept managers, bumbling presidents, and feeble colonels who, despite their posts, do not actually lead. Remember the school principal who "stopped being the educational leader" of his school. Though he held the form of a leader, his spirit was anything but. One can hold the forms of leadership without possessing its spirit.

> *Holding a position of power does not automatically make someone a leader. Positions are forms. Real leadership starts with spirit.*

The *spirit* of leadership is not restricted to people of rank. Some truly powerful leaders don't hold any positional authority. Though they lack leadership's forms, they are suffused with its spirit. Mahatma Gandhi defeated the British Empire though he never held any office or leadership position.

SPIRIT FIRST

True leaders at all levels *put spirit first*. Their allegiance is to spirit, not to form. This is a simple principle, but it demands some explanation. What does it mean, in practical terms, to put spirit first?

Putting spirit first means recognizing that forms are most valuable when they engage spirit. When they hurt spirit, they're dangerous. Forms may be oppressive, like Jim Crow laws, and even good forms can wear out their usefulness. When they do, they no longer express spirit.

We have already described the dangers of remaining invested in such forms. Even "bad" forms can keep you in their grip. Anyone can be stuck in harmful forms because of habit, fear, and apathy.

> *THREE WAYS TO PUT*
> *SPIRIT FIRST*
>
> *1. Be willing to leave behind forms that no longer foster spirit.*
>
> *2. Seek out new forms that enhance spirit.*
>
> *3. Pay continual attention to spirit. Listen to the "experience" of yourself and others.*

The title of this chapter is "Breakthrough Leadership" because real leaders break out of these deadening forms. They don't allow spirit to wither and refuse to accept a transactional culture. Think of Martin, the banker who told his boss that "our meetings are a bunch of BS." He put the needs of his spirit before the pressure to get along with the boss.

One way that leaders "put spirit first" is by abandoning untrustworthy, restrictive, or outgrown forms. For real leaders, spirit is more important than the order and regimentation that form provides.

People can also put spirit first by moving *toward* new, spirit-friendly forms. A leader who's interested in vitality does not demolish forms just to demolish forms. Instead, he searches for forms that enhance spirit. When people talk about a leader with "vision," they mean a vision of new forms that engage spirit.

This doesn't mean that a leader generates all her own visions by herself. Some do, but others work collaboratively. A leader might convene a group with the express purpose of finding a vision, as the university administrators did with their "speaking circles."

Wherever a vision comes from, a leader embraces and helps implement it. She does the hard work of gathering facts, explaining, exhorting, and listening in order to build critical mass. The leader *finds new ways to bring form and spirit together.*

Sometimes a leader creates new, spirit-friendly forms. Sometimes good forms already exist, and the leader helps people understand and engage with those forms. (Good coaches and teachers do the latter—they get people into existing forms. They stimulate their students and explain what they need to do to succeed. They show how to mesh spirit with the form.)

Finally, another way to put spirit first is to actively look for it. We talked in Part One about the importance of dealing not only with "events" but also with people's "experience" of those events. Events happen to forms; experience happens to spirit. What does a change or crisis mean to people? What does it make them think and feel? How does it affect their ability to achieve their goals? Does it mesh with their values and meet their needs?

It's equally important for leaders to pay attention to their own spirits and experience. Often a leader becomes a leader because by speaking from the gut he can articulate what is going on with other people. Martin, the banker, was such a person. In order to say that he felt "covered in blood," he had to pay attention to his own thoughts and ideas and trust they were valid. The danger in making such a statement was not just that he could have infuriated his boss: imagine what would have happened if no one else in the room knew what he was talking about. Martin was bold enough to trust his spirit, and by trusting he articulated a feeling shared by the other executives. Just by speaking from the heart, he reinforced his own authority. Everyone in the room possessed the forms of leadership; Martin asserted its spirit.

> *Leaders must pay attention to their own spirits and experience.*

These are the three primary ways to put spirit first. You leave forms that don't engage spirit and build new forms that do. You make a habit of listening to and trusting experience, your own as well as others.

The irony of this sort of leadership is that you aren't leading so much as following. You follow spirit where it leads.

To follow spirit takes courage, because this means putting your ego and your comfort second. Following spirit will lead to a richer, deeper, more interesting and exciting life. It is a powerful experience, and brings you into closer contact with others and with yourself. To follow the spirit also means you don't have the luxury of letting yourself stay in a rut; spirit frequently calls you to renew yourself and your surroundings.

This chapter is written for those who want to accept the challenge.

THE QUEST FOR CLARITY

The first step toward following spirit is figuring out what spirit "wants." This is not a mystical process. Clarification—setting up "four walls" within which you explore facts, reflect, engage in dialogue, and receive guidance—is really a process of determining what works for spirit and what doesn't. To reach clarity is to discover a new way in which form and spirit can interact.

Clarification is a process of discovering what the spirit "wants." Leaders should make it a habit.

We have spoken about Clarification as a response to a crisis, and it is a very good way of responding to chaos. There will always be times, especially during major transitions, when you need to embark on a big Clarification project. But if you want to follow spirit closely, then ongoing Clarification should become a habit.

An example: a close friend of ours died recently after a long struggle with cancer. She was sad to die, but was consoled, she said, because she had no regrets about her life. A big reason for her lack of regrets was that she always tried to follow her spirit. Every day she took walks with her husband or a friend, and they talked about what they were doing and whether it suited them. Those conversations helped her determine whether her job still engaged her and what she might want to do in the future. She became very sensitive to the needs of her spirit and any problems she had with the forms in her life. As a result, she rarely felt like she was doing anything she didn't want to do. When a new hope or dream occurred to her, she pursued it. When she felt constricted, she worked to change the forms that held her back. She lived a fulfilling life of travel and deep friendships.

Like everyone, she periodically found herself dissatisfied and unhappy, but kept working toward clarity—that is, until she could clearly see what forms would make her spirit feel better.

She did this within her own "four walls." She found safety with people she trusted, and took time and found space apart for reflection and dialogue. When she needed help, she sought it.

We aren't suggesting that you should take walks every day—each person needs to find a method that works for him or her—but rather that our friend was an excellent model of someone who paid attention to her own spirit. (Not coincidentally, she also paid great attention to others' spirits. She was always curious about other people, and her compassion led her to volunteer for the poor and the sick. Being aware of where your spirit is leading you does not mean that you have to become selfish and self-involved. On the contrary, following the spirit brings you into a deeper relationship with the world and people around you.)

In the following sections, we describe how to put spirit first.

THE "FOUR WALLS" IN DAILY LIFE

A university president once told us how he made decisions. "I seek out as many opinions as I can," he said. "I go for as broad a collection of advice as I can find. I listen to everyone, then I go into my office, close the door, and figure out what I want to do.

"The only times I've regretted a decision," he continued, "is when I didn't follow my instincts. If I let someone else influence me too much and make a decision that goes against my own instinct, then if the decision turns out to be the wrong one, I've got no recourse. I *knew* that wasn't the thing to do, but I have to take responsibility for the consequences. I'm content to make a wrong decision if it's *my* decision. I can say, 'All right, it may not have worked out, but at least I was doing what I thought was best.'"

He was doing a type of Clarification. He established the "four walls" of a good form. He gave himself *time* to gather information and make a decision. He "closed the door" to provide himself a *safe*, separate *space* for reflection. If he needed *additional resources* (e.g. money), he obtained them. With this time, space, and safety, he gathered facts, engaged in dialogue, and reflected; he sought guidance if he needed it.

Ultimately, he was *creating the opportunity to listen to his spirit.* That is, to discern what he really thought, felt, and valued. He based his decisions on what he discovered—on the clarity he achieved.

Paying close attention to spirit is something any person can benefit from. Leaders will find it particularly important because it helps them discern problems and opportunities, envision new forms, and make decisions.

A leader is distinguished from a follower because she doesn't just find clarity for herself. She does two additional things. She *acts* on her clarity, moving to implement new ideas and build new forms, and she *helps others reach clarity.* These acts of leadership put spirit first.

> *A leader is distinguished by the fact that she doesn't just find clarity. She also helps others reach clarity, and she acts on her clarity.*

Consider Tom Grand, the bank CEO. As he plotted his bank's expansion, he spent a good deal of time reflecting on and talking about the changes it would bring. He personally had clarity. He also worked to translate his vision into reality: he was creating new forms all over the place. When he asked us to facilitate a workshop, he took the first step toward building the "four walls" for his employees. Once he discovered how confused everyone around him was, he made Clarification for others his first priority. He gave the auditors their retreat. He provided training workshops for every employee of every branch so that each person received guidance, facts, and the opportunity for reflection and dialogue. In short, he made sure his people reached clarity and that the bank's new forms were comprehensible and helpful.

THE CLARIFICATION PROCESS: SUGGESTIONS FOR LEADERS

Once you've established the four walls, Clarification can become an ongoing process, or a special occasion, or both. Whether it's something you do on a regular basis or only in response to a crisis, the same four clarifiers—

reflection, dialogue, facts, and guidance—remain essential. Here is how leaders can use them to their advantage.

Reflection

Reflection means paying attention to what you're thinking and feeling. Reflection is a way of understanding what is happening to forms and spirit. It's a way to identify critical events and discern the meaning of experience, so you can keep form and spirit in sync. Here are examples of questions we've asked people to reflect on. They are good prompts for productive reflection.

Questions to Prompt Reflection

- How are the forms around me working?
- What is my experience of the current situation?
- What is my level of trust in the forms that I often encounter?
- How deeply am I engaged in these forms?
- Should I be investing more or less spirit in these forms than I am?
- What important forms have I neglected? What forms will feed my spirit?
- Where would I like to see myself and my organization in the future? What forms will make that vision possible?
- How much do I trust others in my organization/group?
- What gestures of trust can I make to improve trust around me?
- How are the spirits of my colleagues faring?
- What forms will help their spirits?
- How can I make my organization more reflective and less transactional?
- What forms in my organization need improvement? What can I personally do to improve them?
- If I am in a period of change, what stage am I in—am I losing Form One, building Form Two, or immersed in Chaos?

- What interim forms will help me move from one stage of change to the next?

- How can I improve my organization's "markers of vitality"? (i.e. spontaneous leadership, stewardship, respect for differences, confidence, and lack of ego.)

These questions can get you reflecting effectively. There are countless others, and they all work equally well when starting a dialogue. To reflect on such questions effectively, you need to do three things. First, you need to listen to yourself—your thoughts and feelings—without editing or censoring yourself. Second, you must be patient. And third, you should try to make it a habit. Let's look at each of these practices individually.

> *THREE KEYS TO*
> *REFLECTION*
> *1. Don't censor yourself.*
> *2. Be patient.*
> *3. Make it a habit.*

1. Follow your thoughts and feelings without censoring or editing them.

During reflection, the spirit may present itself in a number of ways. It may pop up as a question: "I wonder why my colleagues can't get along?" or "What if we're looking at this problem the wrong way?" It may appear as an image, a realization, a hunch, or an insight. It may arise as the awareness that you're confused or frustrated.

The important thing is not *how* an idea or feeling arises, but *that* it arises. It's crucial that you allow these notions to appear and follow where they lead *without criticizing them*. Rather than force yourself to feel something you "should" feel, listen to what you do feel.

Most of us have been taught from a young age to be polite, to say only nice things, and not put ourselves out on a limb by saying unorthodox things. Politeness and civility are indeed wonderful, but all too often, people don't let themselves *think* impolite or, especially, unorthodox things.

The spirit may be saying painful things, or things that threaten your daily routines. You may realize that you hate your job or you've missed your true calling as a horse trainer. You may discover that *you* are the source of a problem, or that a difficult situation is partly your fault. Spirit can and often does judge us. It can tell us we're on the wrong track. Following the spirit is not always fun; it's not always whistling in the sunshine.

Whether its lessons are enjoyable or not, reflection means thinking about this fundamental question: *What is going on with me, and what forms might fit my spirit (or my organization's spirit) better?*

2. Be patient.

The key word in reflection is "allow." You need to "allow" ideas and feelings to emerge without censoring them. At the same time, you can't force yourself to understand something. You can't put clarification on a deadline. The harder you push to make your reflection "productive," the more tense you become, and the less likely to hear the quiet insights that reflection often offers.

In our culture, we want everything to perform according to the clock. Clocks and deadlines are forms, and sometimes spirit will fit into a form, and sometimes it won't.

Sometimes an answer only comes after you've given up on it. Probably you've had the experience of thinking endlessly about a problem and failing to come up with a solution. Then, when you're taking a shower or making a sandwich, the answer suddenly blossoms, vivid and whole inside your mind. Clarity doesn't come just because you insist on it.

3. Make reflection a habit.

The more you reflect, the better at it you become. It takes practice to stop censoring yourself while you work patiently toward clarity.

Most of us are so strapped for time that it can be a challenge to set aside a period of reflection every day or even every week. It helps to find gaps in your daily schedule where you're not "on," and don't have to be productive. You might walk to work, so your mind has time to wander. If you drive, don't spend the time on your cell phone or listening to the radio. Instead, let your mind go. You can also take 15 minutes after lunch to muse.

Physical exercise can offer excellent opportunities for reflection. Runners know that after a mile or two, the pressing concerns of the day fade away, replaced by a flow of thoughts. Other exercise can be similarly meditative.

We personally allow ourselves brief periods of reflection each day, simply to process information and "check-in" with ourselves to see how we feel and what we think about the day's events. At work, we might take a quick walk or just scribble some notes to ourselves during a free moment. Other people find other ways of reflecting. Writing in a journal, watching the clouds, driving aimlessly, meditating—all of these can be wonderful tools of reflection.

If we're receptive to spirit, spirit shows up with increasing frequency. If we ignore it, then it may not speak when we suddenly need it to.

DIALOGUE

Reflection alone may not be sufficient to give you clarity, especially with thorny problems. Even if you find clarity about what you personally want to do, you need to communicate that with the people around you. That's where dialogue comes in. Dialogue helps people reflect, because it brings in outside ideas (think of how helpful it is to talk through a problem with a friend). Reflection helps dialogue, because it prepares people for the conversation.

True dialogue is like reflection with more than one person. The "Questions to Prompt Reflection" also spark dialogue, and dialogue works best under the same three conditions important to reflection: avoid censoring, be patient, and make it a habit. When those conditions are met, spirit has a chance to be heard. People tell the truth about what they think and feel; they say important and insightful things. Ideas fly.

The opposite of dialogue is transactional talk. Just as you can have a transactional culture, in which every relationship slides along the surface of things, so you can have a transactional conversation. In transactional conversation, the things people really think and feel never get expressed (though they may get hinted at).

The bankers' workshop is a good example of both transactional talk and real dialogue. The conversation started out transactionally, because the branch presidents refused to talk about anything but the events they had been through. No one would talk openly until at last Martin broke through to the truth with his statement that he felt "covered in blood." A reflective dialogue ensued.

To encourage true dialogue, the first step is to establish an interim form with the "four walls" of time, space apart, guidance, and, above all, safety.

There's another crucial task, especially for leaders: *let go*. Like reflection, dialogue can't be forced. Indeed, "Letting Go" may be the most important thing a leader can do for a dialogue. It is so important that we've come to live by this precept: When a dialogue is not going well, the first task of every participant—especially leaders—is to ask, "What am I holding on to?" Letting go of that thing will free up enormous energy and push the dialogue to new levels.

> *To make dialogue work, leaders have to "let go" of roles and positions, the need for answers, personal agendas, and the fear of chaos.*

What do people have to let go of?

1. Roles and positions. People often feel they have to play a part that fits their role. The boss may believe she can't show any weakness or pessimism. As a result, she'll remain transactional and guarded throughout the conversation. She may feel it's her duty to shoot down anyone who brings in a negative notion. Someone lower in the hierarchy may not speak up because she feels that she's "just a secretary" with nothing to contribute.

2. The need for answers. Most of us hate the feeling of being helpless in the face of a problem, and we're uncomfortable when people bring deep problems to our attention. Our initial reaction—for instance, when someone says "I can't explain this new accounting system to my employees"—is to leap up and offer answers. "Well," we say blithely, "just hire a trainer."

We've mentioned the importance of *identifying themes* in a dialogue. One of the themes may be that everyone is confused or hurt or angry. If you meet their confusion with quick-fix answers, most people aren't going to speak up.

Leaders must remember that following the spirit is not the same thing as trying to Band-Aid every hurt feeling or confused mind.

3. Personal agendas. Nothing kills dialogue faster than a hidden personal agenda. It can be very tough to let go of your agenda. Sometimes it can be hidden even from yourself.

Some examples of personal agendas include the need to be right, to accomplish a pet project, to be the center of attention, and the need to not make waves.

The reason that personal agendas hurt dialogue is that they "load" the conversation. People say things they don't mean, or they don't tell the whole truth. They try to angle and control the conversation, rather than learn from it. They try to squelch anyone who seems to be working against their agenda.

The best way to neutralize personal agendas is simply to make them conscious. Saying that you have a personal agenda, even to yourself, is often enough to break through the ice of transaction and into real dialogue.

4. Fear of chaos. Telling the truth, especially during times of change, often means exposing chaos. People may expose simmering confusion and animosity, turf battles, a long history of grievances, a sense of opportunities lost, or perhaps even of failure. People may be criticized and their ideas reviled.

Just as honest reflection may teach you unpleasant things about yourself and demand that you change, so it is with dialogue. It may be even harder to take because others are telling you these things. It's often easier to take criticism from yourself.

What's more, dialogue among a group in chaos can seem out of control and even counter-productive. When people bring up difficult issues, other people often rush to make the conversation shallow again. "Whew! What about this weather we've been having!"

Getting through chaos can seem impossible, and it's at this time that guidance becomes so important.

5. Unfinished business. In almost every workshop we've ever given, unfinished business ran like a vein of ore through the soil of conversation. For the organization to move forward, people have to let go of it.

This is often hard to do, because talking about unfinished business often means getting into conflict with people. Some people don't want to let go of their unfinished business. They use old grievances as a weapon. They may have a legitimate beef with the organization, but don't try to resolve it. Instead, they keep returning to it, like kids who keep picking their scabs off, preventing the wounds from healing. Whenever they feel threatened, they cling to their unfinished business and refuse to change.

On the other hand, people who keep repeating their grievances may feel they are not being heard, and keep repeating the message in the hope that they'll get through. The crucial step in resolving unfinished business is to make sure that everyone is heard. If you're the one with unfinished business, tell people you need to be understood. If it's someone else, listen carefully—and most important, show you've understood by repeating to them, *in your own words*, what you think they've said.

FACTS

When people talk about facts, they're usually talking about numbers, specific events, or the bottom line. These facts are important, but if they were the only important facts, most of the crises we've described in this book wouldn't have happened. There are more elusive, human facts, such as the history of an organization and its culture. People's experiences are facts.

Sometimes even falsehoods can be facts. For instance, all the employees of a small company believed the president was having an affair with one of their co-workers. This wasn't true, but what was true was that they believed it, and their belief affected the entire company. (When facts are in short supply, rumors aren't. People want to know what's going on around them, and if they don't know the truth, stories and rumors will fill the vacuum. The problem with these stories and rumors floating around is they are usually much uglier than the truth. For some reason, the stories that catch on tend to be ugly, paranoid ones.)

We have identified four categories of fact: economic and legal realities, organizational history, processes, and people issues.

1. Economic and legal realities.

When people think of facts, they usually think of these realities. Bottom-line numbers fit in here, along with legal obligations to customers and shareholders, trade laws, and laws governing union relations. This category also includes internal policy and regulations, and ethics, too: most organizations are constrained from certain practices by their ethical sense.

2. Organizational history.

The history of an organization is a vital fact. Remember the school principal who "quit being the educational leader of the school"? Union representatives and administrators battled through several rounds of contract negotiations and consistently failed to reach accommodation, leaving the teachers without any contract at all. Though there was genuine conflict over pay scales and benefits, there were deeper conflicts involved as well. That school's history was rife with conflict and failure. Only when this history was uncovered and put to rest could the school community really come together again.

This is why we emphasize recapitulation. We ask people to tell us their stories about the organization. We ask them whether they know the organization's history. Do they understand how the organization got to where it is? Recapitulation offers a chance to put unresolved aspects of that history to rest.

3. Processes.

It was a well-intentioned but painfully naïve group. Young and excitable, they worked in the local branch of a national nonprofit. One day, at the end of a routine daily meeting, one of them offered a proposal to their boss. "We'd like a four-day work week," she announced.

The boss assumed she was kidding and laughed.

She wasn't kidding and his laughter rankled. "That's so disrespectful," she complained.

"Wait," said the boss. "You're *serious*? You want a four-day week?"

Six other employees nodded. They had been discussing the matter for a week. They worked hard, they said, and they deserved full pay and benefits for a shorter work-week.

It's not hard to imagine where their proposal ended up. Part of the problem was that the employees had failed to consider the organization's economic facts. Even if the boss had wanted to meet their desires, the bottom line wouldn't allow it.

They had also fatally ignored the organization's processes. Specifically, they had brought up the proposal in the wrong forum and in the wrong way. A daily update meeting is no place to propose radical change, and such a proposal shouldn't be offered with an offhand comment.

This story points out the importance of paying attention to process. Each organization is full of processes. There are manufacturing processes and payroll processes, hiring and firing processes, and, of course, decision-making processes.

Good leaders work to understand the organization's processes—both operational processes like manufacturing and financial, and human relations processes, like who needs to communicate with whom, and who makes decisions and how.

People who don't respect such processes will have a hard time trying to be leaders. Their ideas won't stand a chance against the wall of "We just don't *do* that."

4. People.

It may sound strange to think of people as facts, but they are. So are all the things that come with them: their experience, knowledge, emotions, values, and relationships. These facts influence an organization more than any other. If you want to understand an organization's facts, you have to understand its people, plain and simple.

Talking about people's experiences and recapitulating their history is not "soft" or peripheral to the hard world of fact. People are the most important of facts. Vitality can't be accomplished without understanding them.

GUIDANCE

Gordon Burns, the head of the agricultural firm mentioned in the introduction, explained why he hired us to help him. "I knew I was doing something wrong," he said, "but I didn't know what. And I didn't know what to do about it."

Leaders give and receive guidance. We've talked about the importance of following spirit, and we'll reiterate here that the best guidance usually comes from one's own spirit. But figuring out what the spirit wants is often a difficult task, and sometimes, as in Gordon Burns' case, the spirit is simply adrift.

Whether you want to *be* a guide or *find* a guide, we suggest these qualities of a good guide:

1. Be safe.

A good guide keeps confidential matters confidential. A good guide listens without judging (just as you need to reflect and dialogue without censorship, so you need a guide who won't censor).

2. Be honest and respectful.

A good guide is honest. She speaks the truth and is careful to do so respectfully. Truth that tramples feelings doesn't help. Honesty and respect, moreover, can also be shown in how a guide listens. How can you be an honest listener? Be willing to listen to uncomfortable truths, and accept or at least consider constructive criticism.

3. Go deep.

Get beyond transactional conversation by talking about experience. Pursue the truth, even if you don't know what the truth is.

4. Be neutral or find someone who is.

Whenever you have a direct stake in an issue, especially a conflict, it helps to bring in an outside guide. Outsiders are not only neutral, but when they do the work of mediating a meeting or asking questions, you are free to do your own reflection and participate in dialogue and fact-finding.

SPONTANEOUS LEADERSHIP: VITALITY IN ACTION

We'd like to share one last story to demonstrate the spirit of leadership. Some of the most effective leaders we've ever worked with did not possess much positional authority. They were the volunteer members of the "Next Step Task Force," a group of schoolteachers who came together to lead their school through a difficult developmental change.

At the task force's school, the problems were systemic and ongoing. Most serious was a crisis of leadership from the top. A series of principals had come and gone, each one staying only long enough to undo what the others had done before quitting or being ousted. The turnover had given many members of the school an inferiority complex: why didn't anyone want to stay there?

Part of the answer was that while each principal was greener than the last, the faculty was dominated by a group of entrenched, cynical veterans. Suspicious of most authority, the old-timers seemed to trust only the union, of which they themselves were representatives. There were other problems as well. The school building had been poorly planned, isolating small groups of classrooms from one another. Making matters worse, the building now had to house a greatly-increased student body after budget considerations forced the school to merge with another.

When yet another new principal came aboard, it looked as if the same old story would soon repeat itself: idealistic new administrator comes in with high hopes and no sense of history, suspicious faculty pounce on her inevitable missteps and make her life miserable.

This didn't happen. A group of teachers and staff members—most of them younger, but still a good cross-section of the school—had seen enough of those battles. Their reaction was both brave and sane. Rather than getting caught up in efforts to break the new principal or to force the jaded faculty to embrace her, they gave themselves a simple mission: to do what they could to improve the school. They followed their spirits' demand for new forms.

The task force was an interim form. It met on school grounds after hours, and provided the "four walls"—their meetings gave them time and a place. They worked out a contract for safety, and rustled up other re-sources when they needed them.

Equally important, the interim form bypassed some old, ineffec-tive forms. One of those forms was the old relationship between the administration and the faculty. That relationship was defined by ani-mosity between young principals and veteran union leaders. The new form let people collaborate on problems they all cared about. As task force reps, the participants were equal; their job titles didn't get in the way of dialogue.

Inside that interim form, the task force pursued clarity. First they set out some open-ended questions to reflect on and discuss. What should be the school's "next step"? How would they improve faculty/staff relations? How could they make the best of the building's awkward layout? Were there better ways to serve the larger student body?

They invited everyone in the school community (from teachers and administrators to parents and janitors) to join them. In this way, the task force began paving the way toward critical mass. Moreover, they made particular overtures to the principal. They wanted her involvement so that she'd feel welcome at the school and engaged in the process. They also un-derstood the facts of the school's processes: unless they got the principal's support, none of their suggestions would go anywhere.

They gathered facts when they needed them, and they hired us for guidance.

One of the things we admired about the task force was its patience. The group moved very carefully, one step at a time. From the moment they first started meeting, they told people what they were doing and why. They took small, humble steps, and didn't attempt a revolution or coup. They weren't out to change the school top to bottom. They were just meeting to talk, gather ideas, and in the end, they'd write up their findings for the school board to consider.

Contrast their patience with the "shoot first, aim later" mentality of the people who wanted a four-day work week. The task force never made such a radical proposal; they moved carefully enough that no one was alienated. Certainly some old union hands were suspicious, and the administration held off on its approval for a while, but the group kept trying to earn the benefit of the doubt.

Meanwhile, the task force was quietly building a foundation for serious change. People invested spirit into the task force and, for the first time in years, became optimistic about the school's chances. A few small victories built their confidence. Before long, people throughout the school community began to believe that real, deep change might be possible.

In the midst of all this, a fascinating thing happened. The spontaneous leaders in the task force, who had little positional authority, *made their bosses better leaders*. The principal gained credibility as she and the task force members got to know each other. She learned facts about the school's history, processes, and people—and soon she was taking this into consideration when she made decisions. She was also able to communicate her own facts, ideas, and emotions to the faculty and staff. They understood her better and respected her more, even when they disagreed with her. The hostility drained out of faculty/administration relations, and as the task force built momentum, the cynical community members who were unwilling to change gradually became less and less powerful.

(This is not to say that the task force deserves all the credit for making the principal more effective. She herself showed great leadership by acknowledging and encouraging the task force from the beginning. Many bosses would feel threatened even by the task force's incremental steps or wouldn't know how to handle its enthusiasm. To her credit, she saw the value of letting the "volunteers" on the task force do their thing.)

The result of their efforts was a report, distributed to the rest of the school faculty, suggesting possible improvements to the school. The task force asked the other teachers to consider the report and give their own reactions and suggestions. With those responses in hand, they revised the report and distributed it through the school community and to the school board.

While the report went a long way toward renewing the school's forms and rejuvenating its spirit, the task force itself made the biggest impact on vitality. The process of developing the report opened dialogue and built trust in a place where suspicion and cynicism had thrived. Not only did the task force members become a cohesive unit—crossing barriers between staff, administration, and faculty—but the group also reached out to the community. It offered a place for volunteers to engage, and gave people a voice. The task force listened to the experiences of other school employees, students, parents, and taxpayers. People believed their opinions mattered; they knew they could participate in the life of the school.

Once it had presented its proposals to the school board, the task force disbanded. Like all good interim forms, it didn't try to outlive its usefulness. It had served its purpose—to recommend positive, developmental changes—and once that purpose had been fulfilled, the team members went back to their regular jobs.

Of everyone we've had the great pleasure of working with, these were among our favorites. We were continually moved by the way they trusted and followed their spirits. We loved their optimism, faith, courage, and, above all, leadership. They brought form and spirit together in remarkable ways. People like them are indispensable sources of vitality. It's been our great honor to work with them, and other clients from Gordon Burns to staff members at the government agency, and everyone in between. It's our hope that this book will help you find the vitality they possess.

BIBLIOGRAPHY

Bridges, William. *Transitions: Making Sense of Life's Changes* (Reading, MA: Addison-Wesley, 1980).

Hugo, Richard. "Letter to Matthews from Barton Street Flat," *Collected Poems* (New York: W. W. Norton & Co., 1979).

Levi, Primo, and Philip Roth. "A Conversation with Primo Levi," *Survival in Auschwitz* (New York: Collier Books, 1993).

Loehr, James E. *Toughness Training for Life* (New York: Plume/Penguin, 1994).

May, Rollo. *The Courage to Create* (New York: Bantam Books, 1978).

Peters, Thomas J. and Robert H. Waterman, Jr. *In Search of Excellence* (New York: Harper and Row, 1982).

Schama, Simon. "Balmorality," *The New Yorker*, August 11, 1997.

Watterson, Bill. *Something Under the Bed is Drooling: A Calvin and Hobbes Collection* (Kansas City: Andrews and McMeel, 1988).

Wetlaufer, Suzy. "After the Layoffs, What Next?" *Harvard Business Review*, September–October 1998.

Wright, Richard, "The Ethics of Living Jim Crow," *Uncle Tom's Children* (New York: HarperPerennial, 1993).

ABOUT THE AUTHORS

DR. CARL (CHUCK) LOFY is a professional consultant and trainer. His began his professional career as a Jesuit priest, earning his doctorate at Innsbruck University in Austria and Gregorian University in Rome. Upon leaving the Jesuits, he spent more than twenty years as a university professor and administrator, holding such positions as vice president for student services and interim vice president for academic affairs. He later co-founded and directed the Wellness Center of Minnesota, where he counseled patients and taught managers to lead their organizations through transitions. Demand for his expertise encouraged him to establish Lofy Associates—a consulting firm specializing in change, trust-building, and revitalization—with his wife, Mary. He is the author of a collection of speeches, "A Grain of Wheat" and of a collection of audio tapes, "Conversations with Dr. Chuck Lofy."

DR. MARY MEAD LOFY has been a consultant, speaker, and trainer for Lofy Associates for fifteen years. A long-time community leader, she has extensive experience in teaching, business, and politics. She holds a doctorate in Human and Organizational Systems from the Fielding Graduate Institute in Santa Barbara, California. Early in her career, she was a Dominican nun and taught in primary and secondary schools. For nine years, she was a partner in a retail gift shop, and for fifteen she served on the board of Norwest Bank in Mankato, Minnesota. Her community activities include two terms as an elected member of the Mankato City Council and long-term involvement with the United Way, the YMCA, the Minnesota Heart Health Program, and other organizations. For these activities she has been awarded the YWCA Leadership Award for Women; the Nicholas J. Coleman Award; and the Martin Luther King, Jr., Pathfinder Award.

JOHN LOFY is a writer living in Ann Arbor, Michigan. The author of fiction, essays, and feature journalism, he has won several awards and fellowships for his writing. He has also taught English at the University of Michigan, where he received an MFA in creative writing.